Business Box Set

Ross Elkins

Table of Contents

Leadership

Elevate Yourself and Those around You

Influence, Business Skills, Coaching & Communication

Disclaimer Notice:

Please note the information contained within this document is for educational and entertainment purposes only. Every attempt has been made to provide accurate, up to date and reliable complete information. No warranties of any kind are expressed or implied. Readers acknowledge that the author is not engaging in the rendering of legal, financial, medical or professional advice.

Introduction

What makes a leader? There is an old standing debate, about whether leaders are born or made. Some people possess the inherent qualities of a good leader, while others have to cultivate such qualities. However, there is no rule that declares natural leaders better than those who have honed their skills to match those required of a leader. In the corporate world, leadership is one of the most sought-after qualities in an employee. In a managerial position, you are expected to handle a team, nurture them, motivate them, inspire them and ensure the best possible outcome and productivity from the team. All this cannot be achieved without possessing the skills of a strong leader.

Leadership can be defined as the process of influencing the behaviour of one's subordinates, without making them feel like they are working under a dictator. It is the social process of directing people in the way that you see fit, helping them visualize a common goal and invoking the drive to achieve it. Leadership is about bringing people together, and harnessing their abilities into a joint effort to achieve a significant vision.

A good leader is able to identify problems and then prescribe a strategic plan to deal with the same. Leaders are expected to push the boundaries of their corporate setting, see the bigger picture and emerge with a mission that you are going to work towards achieving. Leaders are different from managers in the way that while manager's focus on supervising their subordinates and managing problems, leaders focus on motivating their subordinates into overcoming problems, and seek out issues for change.

Leaders are not built overnight. If you want to act as an effective leader, someone that people will look up to, you must allow yourself to constantly evolve. You must allow the constant change in global trends and workforce diversity factor into the way you deal with people. Leadership is about making effective decisions without arousing conflict among the employees.

In this book, we discuss the finer nuances of what makes a good leader, strategies for leading in business, expectations and demands, among other things.

Chapter 1

Qualities of an Effective Leader

Some people are born with an innate sense of leadership, and are good at making effective managerial decisions and leading their co-workers to maximum productivity, while others need a nudge in the right direction to realize their full potential when it comes to leadership.

If you occupy a managerial position in business, it is expected of you to take effective decisions and lead people in order to fulfill the visions and goals of the company. Knowing how to lead, to influence, and to communicate effectively are the prerequisites for anybody in a position where they are responsible for the growth of a company.

There are many a qualities that are essential for being a good leader. Some are inborn, some need to be developed and nurtured. The characteristics of a good leader involve:

Confidence and Self-Assurance

Since leaders are responsible for the outcome of the group, it is prudent for them to be absolutely sure about the decisions they make. A confident approach and a strong belief in self are inspiring traits; group members are more likely to follow someone who is willing to tackle a problem head-on with confidence and unwavering spirit. Leaders who are sure that they are making the right decisions, and do not seek approval show resilience. Confident leaders command respect and inspire people to follow them.

To make a proper distinction, the respect that leaders command comes from embodying the example and not solely by giving orders. This is where inspiration develops in others. When they see a person exemplify the task or skill at hand, they are more inclined to attempt it themselves, and then they become willing to follow and contribute to that person's directive in future endeavours and the larger scheme.

All other skills outlined in this book are rendered moot for the aspiring leader until they have cultivated or naturally possess the confidence necessary to take on the role. And confidence does not have to be this mystical seed for growing prosperity and influence either. If you think back to when you were a child and just went ahead and did things without contemplating all the 'what if's,' you will find that most all of us have always possessed this quality and while some have forgotten they have it, others have just had more practice at exercising it over the years.

To cultivate confidence where it may appear to be lacking, a person has to tend to the thoughts in their mind like a garden. They must identify any and every thought that exhibits self-doubt without trying to reason or justify why it's there and simply uproot it. Get rid of it, because there is absolutely no service a self-doubting thought can provide, other than a false sense of safety that actually prevents one from being themselves and their best. A person must then tend to the positive thoughts they have about themselves and nurture them so that they grow along with their already noticeable traits. One must also plant seeds of positive thoughts in their fertile mind of how they see themselves at their best and even qualities they feel they don't currently exhibit but aspire to have. For habitual self-doubters this may require a 'fake it till you make it' approach. However, this process involves directly changing one's mindset which will require ample amounts of practice and repetition no matter who the person is.

With time, enforcing those positive thoughts will begin give way to revealing themselves in personal behavior, and every external challenge that contends with those thoughts is a chance to exert one's confidence with both assertion and humility. Humility in the sense that one is not weak, but quite the opposite, they are humble because they are sure of themselves without having to prove it.

Like the simple phrase, 'monkey see, monkey do', *be* the example, set the standard and others will be compelled to recognize it and live up to it.

Good communication skills

How you perform as a leader is heavily dependent on your ability to communicate with the team. A good leader is able to outline project objectives, state problems, and chart strategies, all in a very precise manner that leaves no room for error or confusion. At the end of the day, the group leader is held accountable for the merits or demerits of the team, so the leader is expected to make sure that there is no lapse in understanding what a particular project entails.

This is why communication skills are crucial and perhaps under-appreciated in the cache of leadership resources. Of course it would be ideal to present a project plan to a team then immediately set it into motion, however a leader must deal with different perspectives and interpretations from team members. So while precise presentation is foremost in communication, there are a few other tactics to solidify a team's understanding as a unit.

Good communicators are good listeners, often paraphrasing what the speaker said and checking in to ensure that they did not misinterpret the message. Ending a briefing or task delegation with concept-checking questions is a good way to ensure that a team member understands what is expected of him or her, and to pinpoint any areas that are not understood so that they may be clarified.

Neuro Linguistic Programming, or NLP, is a study that is becoming more and more popular among leaders in business, education, and other organizations. 'Neuro' refers to the applications and stimulation of the mind, 'Linguistic' speaks to the language we use, whether it is verbal or nonverbal, and 'Programming' suggests the patterns of thinking and behaviour that we become accustomed to operating under.

We will cover more about NLP in Chapter 3. For now, let us simply go over what it may provide for us in a leadership position. By employing NLP, not only when engaging others but in training our minds to think differently as well, we may better develop our communication skills; set convincing and approachable goals for ourselves and others; attain and nurture an increased self-awareness and awareness of others; gain an increased ability to influence and motivate others; and better manage both personal and team performance.

NLP is used more often in leadership coaching and pertains directly to understanding Emotional Intelligence so that the work environment may run more smoothly, as workers will become more apt to feel supported.

Emotional Stability

A good leader is someone who does not let emotions cloud their judgment. An effective leader must, at all times, be ready to take on stress and turmoil, without giving into it and letting frustration affect their decision-making power. This sounds easy enough until the stress actually hits. There are many subtle ways that emotions can impact the decision-making process, so it becomes a leader's responsibility to manage a certain level of awareness within themselves.

Emotional suppression is a common side effect of placing business and business-related tasks first, although it ultimately resurfaces in many different forms. Some of these forms may manifest as physical health issues such as high blood pressure, headaches, or chronic muscle tension. They may include subtle behavioral changes like aloofness, short temper, or disconnection from employees or oneself, which may result in losing focus on higher objectives.

Therefore, emotional stability in the high-stress business environment becomes a kind of dance where a leader must learn to exercise executive judgement in allowing themselves to feel their emotions without being carried away by them. Neither bottling them up, a leader may develop emotional strength to their advantage, using it as fuel for directives and problem solving. For example when a person becomes frustrated, without letting it cloud their judgement they may use that feeling as a drive to do something about the situation at hand rather than just sitting on it. Consider the famous quote, "Within every problem lies opportunity."

In a managerial position, when you are responsible for the outcome of a group, for taking well-meaning decisions, you cannot let anxiety, frustration, fatigue or other such emotional factors get to you. You must be well prepared to tackle high levels of stress and be emotionally equipped to ensure the same for those working with you.

Boldness

A common trait among good leaders is their social aggressiveness and risk-taking nature. While making corporate decisions, sometimes it is required that you take the plunge and go for a risky option that may potentially pay off really well. In such situations, a good leader weighs their options and does not shy away from taking a risk.

Richard Branson, founder of the company Virgin, personifies this quality by enterprising upon virtually every business sector in which he gets involved. Branson's company has invested its efforts in music, cellphones, airlines, railways, and even space shuttles. He is one who will not shy away from a risky venture and has seen his audacity pay off over and over again. Branson is one to advocate for following your gut when appropriate. When you feel strongly about it, sometimes you just have to go for it and take the risk. Sometimes that means investing yourself in a big way, but the rewards can be even bigger.

Good leaders don't let fear control them, their actions, or those of their employees. Fear breeds anxiety among a number of other production-depreciative emotions that hinder progress and pinch off the lifeblood of a company. It is better to face fearful realities courageously than bury heads in the sands of blind work. Courage can be found in the workplace on multiple levels; it doesn't just have to be shown when investing in risky adventures.

Leaders show boldness when they must have conversations with employees, superiors and competitors that require an unattractive truth to be revealed and discussed. They are also bold when having a necessary conversation where they do not have all the answers. Many leaders feel they are expected to have all the answers, so when such a situation arises where they are unprepared, you might find them slinking away from handling it forthright. A good demonstration of this kind of boldness in practice is when leaders encourage pushback from their employees and create an atmosphere for constructive debate where better answers are sure to surface.

It may seem negligible as a quality of boldness, but giving credit to others when so many leaders are image conscious and performance driven is an admirable, courageous trait. This is an exertion of honor among truly great leaders who accept the responsibilities of their position by taking the blame for their team members and giving them credit.

Empathy

The ability to put oneself in someone else's shoes is one of the traits of a good leader. Empathy is a big part of making executive decisions. Being empathetic does not mean that you are too sensitive or let emotions affect you - it simply means that you are able to visualize a situation or an outcome from a different standpoint.

The ability to see a situation from various perspectives is a virtually priceless asset. It is a part of what sets good leaders apart from excellent ones. The more that a leader is able to ascertain the viewpoints of their team members, the better equipped he or she becomes in maintaining compliance of the overall objective. The team will be more attentive because they will feel that their respect for the leader's guidance is reciprocated.

Leaders who show empathy provide a sense to their workers of being heard. Workers who feel they've been heard gain self-satisfaction which they may then transform into a boost in confidence in their work and security among the workplace. Empathy elicits a tendency to work harder because those who receive it feel a stronger connection to the giver of it and may even feel they owe their extra effort to the leader as an expression of gratitude for being understood and respected.

Empathy is a great tool for building trust, and trust is a key factor in smooth running of a team in business. Without trust, your subordinates will never willingly follow your approach or decisions. Being empathetic helps in achieving a good insight into a matter and thus, making better decisions.

Charisma

Influencing people, making them obey your command, ensuring that they follow you - these aren't easy goals to achieve. Leaders should be able to invoke a feeling of motivation and awe in their subordinates, and that comes through charisma.

Charisma involves a creative approach to tasks and to people. It requires the projection of oneself as genuine while being so well organized that that authenticity provides a welcome, fluid candor to every interaction. It is the idea that a professional may be so on top of their game that they make challenges look easy. We see it from star athletes in sports highlights, and in the workplace from people who radiate a kind of magnetism.

Having charisma lends to the idea that while a leader has organized and clarified a plan, is monitoring the progress of the objectives and the members carrying them out, and forecasting future endeavours, he or she is able to maintain a comfortable attitude that is also invigorating for others, a feeling that can't help but influence others to feel better about themselves and their work.

Charismatic leaders are the ones who can be entrusted with turning a company around or going forward into unknown territory with a crack idea for a new product or new business strategy. Charisma is supported by a strong sense of confidence that is so important to leadership, the kind that draws people to follow their lead and trust in their decisions even if they appear bleak at first. And then it would be that charming quality of charisma that a leader would exert to sway the doubtful as well.

This does not all just come from a feather in the cap though. Charismatic leaders operate with a gloss over an internal system of highly strategic thinking, empathetic accordance with their associates, and an eye for detail in reading their environment well, then possibly using that information to their advantage.

To lead people, you must have a strong vision, which can capture the attention of people and unite them into working towards a specific goal. Good leaders entice their subordinates with suitable rewards and incentives and push them into the right direction.

Assertiveness

A good leader always has a dominant personality. Can you picture someone who makes decisions, and is easily swayed into changing them due to the opinions of others, in a successful managerial position? The answer is no.

How does a leader balance themselves between being assertive and pushy? They take the time to develop genuine relationships with team members. Ask about their goals in the workplace and what they would like to work on for themselves personally. Then good leaders will actually share about themselves, communicating what their own goals are and how they feel about changes. They engage in establishing a good rapport from the very beginning and maintain strong relationships. Later on, leaders will be able to use their influence with these relationships to delegate difficult tasks without meeting much, if any, resistance.

Successful leaders will gather as much information as possible to gain a wide, clear perspective before taking action. This sharpens their good judgement so they are perceived as level-headed and fair. Then if their workers feel it appropriate to challenge their way of thinking, the leader can show grace by being open to discussion and allow better decisions to emerge, instantaneously winning them back respect.

If a leader is keen on enforcing their point of view, then they must walk the walk, so to speak, to back it up. If they can prove their assertion by action and example, there will be no one to refute them. Consider in this way that when a leader comes off as curt, they may also be exacting a sense of transparency. Some people will appreciate the straightforward talk without candy coating the message.

In this sense, tactful communication becomes a prized element for an effective, assertive leader. If the leader can exhibit themselves in a range of emotions, even those such as frustration and anger, while maintaining professional respect with their employees, they will furnish themselves as openly human. This quality, which is difficult to maintain within an authoritative position, goes to inspire those working for them.

A good leader is always firm in their approach to both decision making and their dealings with others. To evolve and perform as a leader in the business world, one must be assertive, and not a pushover.

Open to new things

Good leaders are always evolving, both in their outlook and the way they deal with things. A good leader is always open to new ideas, judgment, strategies and policies. An open, broad outlook on things inspires better decision making. Good leaders are always on their feet, thinking up new ideas, getting to know about the latest technologies, or plans that might help the business. The willingness to learn new things will manifest in your subordinates as well, as they look up to you, and the outcome will be a sharper and more efficient taskforce.

Listening skills

While it is essential that a good leader is assertive, it does not mean that they are obstinate about their decisions and do not even accept valid suggestions that might be useful to the business. A good leader is almost always also a good listener, as it is important to take your employees' opinions and insight into account.

Listening to your employees' opinions can offer different perspectives that, even as the versatile and observant leader that you are, perhaps you have not considered yet. They may be able to enrich the dynamic of the workplace so that more employees are satisfied on a matter that you may have overlooked. They may be able to offer insight into troubleshooting or flagging problems with a business procedure or project stage that could save you and your company ample time and money.

Employees in the past have garnered great success for their company because their superior had taken notice of them. The well-known story in the business world of 3M Company's stumble on the invention of the Post-it note is one such example. This has become the quintessential example of innovation for big businesses because although it happened all the way back in 1968 and took 12 years before it was actually marketed, there are very few other examples.

Spencer Silver, a chemist for 3M, was in the developmental stages of creating better adhesives. When he stumbled across a technology involving microspheres that formed a weak adhesive yet retained its stickiness so it could be pulled off and reapplied, he then had the trouble of finding a practical use for it. It was only after he got into talks with a coworker of his, Art Fry, that Post-it note development began.

Fry's problem was that he would bookmark his hymnal book for church choir practice with slips of paper, but when he would go to use the book the paper bookmarks fell out and he would lose his place. He remembered Silver's adhesive and began collaborating with Silver. Many other colleagues were doubtful that any success would come out of Fry's and Silver's developments together. They kept lobbying the idea until after extensive market testing in 1980, 3M released it on the market. The Post-it was an instant hit – a product nobody thought they needed until they did.

An efficient leader is aware of the needs and grievances of his employees, and does not dismiss them when they feel the need to talk about something that pertains to the professional realm. An unwavering refusal to listen to employees would eventually lead to feelings of disrespect and loss of motivation. Paying attention to such grievances may lead to surprising advancements in company infrastructure, innovation development, and even prevention of huge company losses or failure.

Ability to deal with failure

Risk taking, corporate gambles, and decisions that fall short of the mark are a part of being a leader. Sometimes your hard work just doesn't pay off. In such situations, a good leader is one who doesn't get rattled easily. A good leader is someone who is not discouraged or disheartened by failure, and chooses to focus on the next task at hand without letting their failures affect their judgment.

Failure can occur in a number of places along the path of project investment and execution. A good leader should be able to pinpoint where along this spectrum a failure occurred and have the wherewithal to deal with it and/or learn from it accordingly so that it can be avoided in the future.

The key issue is the leader's capability to determine the root cause of a failure, going beyond transparent reasons of the problem. This approach may seem unnecessarily drawn out or tedious to others. However, a disciplined leader will understand that the value of weeding out problematic root causes will ensure less future setbacks or roadblocks and more stable future successes. It is the difference of focusing on the short-term and the long haul, and again, involves seeing the opportunity amidst the challenge.

A leader's attitude toward failure is a defining quality that should not only send the appropriate message to his or her subordinates to keep them from getting entangled in drawbacks, but should also shape their approach and expectations by keeping them aware of what exactly it is that they are pursuing.

This means that for leaders in entrepreneurial ventures and research facilities, failure can be seen as a good thing because the information derived from a setback can be used to get closer to setting the right foot forward. In contrast, leaders in already well-established businesses such as manufacturing companies would more likely view a failure as some internal problem for which they are responsible.

Because so many employees, including those in mid-management and even executive positions, are reluctant to convey bad news to their superiors, failure can often go unnoticed until it is too late. That is why a leader who encourages his or her subordinates to highlight problematic issues immediately will be more successful than one who declares they do not want to hear bad news.

Admitting one's failures, not resorting to the blame game are marks of a good leader. Employees are more likely to follow someone who owns up to his mistakes and takes responsibility for them than someone who wastes precious time in mudslinging.

Chapter 2

What is Expected of a Good Leader?

If you are in a leadership position there are a lot of goals for you to meet, but no matter what the job, the basic expectations from a good leader remain the same. It is said that recognizing passion, authenticity, integrity, and ethics are the four cornerstones of effective leadership. They become personal approaches learned and developed from applying oneself in a situational basis, not just from studying other leaders elsewhere.

It means that you must know yourself thoroughly, unafraid to confront what you may not like to see within yourself. Only then may you find the foundation to lay these cornerstones and bring about an effective change to your surroundings.

Integrity

A good leader is one who puts the needs of the company above his, at all times. Integrity is a defining trait of a good leader; people tend to respect a leader who is devoted to the company and pulls all stops to make sure that the image of the company is not compromised at any cost. Honesty towards the company and the workforce is an endearing and rather appealing quality to have.

Integrity comes with a few affirmations that a leader must live by. Because leaders are essentially role models for the rest of the people – and not just their workforce, but the company itself – it should go without saying that their word is their bond. That means they must follow through with their promises and think carefully about how they conduct themselves and their words to others. Once a leader makes a promise, they live by it.

A leader who breaks their promise s or lies in turn begins to plant seeds of distrust, doubt, and resentment in the minds of their workers. It is not just trust lost in their leader; workers will lose their sense of commitment to the job. Eventually these leaders will reap what they sow when they see morale deteriorate, disharmony pervade in the workplace and efficiency begin to fall apart. Accountability is lost. Workers will lose respect for the company and either leave or slack in their job. This can also mean losing customers.

Cutting corners and cheating may have a temporary appeal for those tempted to take the fast track to success, although it is a short road and others will always catch on eventually. It becomes a case of not just failing oneself, but taking everybody else down too.

Telling the truth with consistency takes guts. It is not for the squeamish who are not able to confront people with bad news. It is important to be straightforward at all times and if at all possible, be prepared with a plan to counteract or bounce back from that bad news – integrity of mission. A good leader has a clear mind to face any situation as it really is without twisting or hoping it to be something else. It is called the reality principle.

Having the clarity to see a situation, good or bad, for what it really is, the grace to admit it to oneself and the integrity to keep everyone they are leading on the same page is what truly wins the loyalty of those working for you. They will be much more persuaded to get behind your course of action, provide constructive criticism, and help find realistic solutions.

Good Communication

Previously we discussed the importance of good communication between a leader and their subordinates. Good communication involves not just speech, but also body language. You want to make sure that the messages your body gives off are the same messages that you are intending with your words and your thoughts. Just as actions speak louder than words, body language is most often a dead giveaway as to what you are actually thinking and feeling regardless of your words.

Take note of your posture right at this very moment. If you are hunching, you have your legs crossed, you are holding your arms, or basically making yourself smaller in any way, it is a telltale sign of introversion. You are closing yourself off in some way, and people take note of this even on the most subtle of subconscious levels. Poor posture and closing oneself off speak to lower levels of confidence and a lower sense of power.

Conversely, open postures such as holding the hands on the hips, relaxing the hands behind the head, standing or sitting with legs further apart and so on are known as power postures. These natural postures establish dominance, one of the traits of a leader, and are even recognized in the animal kingdom. They exert a sense of confidence, engagement, and willingness.

Interestingly enough, studies have shown that by practicing these power poses for a given length of time, the body's physiology reacts to support a higher sense of confidence by an increase in testosterone levels in both men and women and a decrease in cortisol levels, which is a stress hormone.

Tests have been conducted by Amy Cuddy, a social psychologist, along with others, where people would be assigned to practice either high power poses or low power poses for five minutes before taking a high-stress job interview where they were recorded, judged, and given no nonverbal feedback from the interviewers (blank stares). Coders, who were not aware what interviewees practiced which poses beforehand, then watched the tapes of the interviews and decided which people they would like to hire.

Sure enough, all the interviewees who had practiced the high power poses beforehand were chosen for hire and evaluated in high regard. The cause was not so much the content of their speech as it was the candidates' *presence*. The coders described them as appearing more confident, passionate, enthusiastic, authentic, captivating, and comfortable – ALL qualities and traits embodied by great leaders.

This goes to show that while some people may naturally possess leadership qualities and others must work to achieve them, the engaging personal aspects of a motivating, approachable type of leader can be learned and practiced through these power postures for one.

A good leader has a commanding personality, so make sure that you make good eye contact and adopt a firm handshake, among other physical gestures. Very often, it is the non-verbal physical gestures that form an impression of you in someone's head. Good body language is very important in terms of being a good leader.

Analytical thinking

People in a decision making position of authority need to evaluate a problem from all possible outlooks before arriving at a decision. Leaders must analyze the information they are provided, and make key decisions only once they are sure about how it would affect the business right away and in the future as well. While making a decision, a good leader must consider other areas of business as well, so that growth is not severely hindered in a separate department.

Leaders need to adopt a kind of 'Renaissance man' (or woman) attitude. They need to focus on becoming well-rounded and diverse in their capabilities and interests to increase the volume of potential resources and idea pools to draw upon. Lane Wallace of the *New York Times* explained that problem solving should be tackled from a multicultural platform, drawing upon academia, business, the arts and history.

When businesses focus on crunching numbers alone, looking for profits, they leave out not just the critical thinking aspect but a sense of quality too. W. Edwards Deming noticed this and tried to persuade American businesses for years back in the 1940s to make some crucial changes about their attitudes in his 14 key principles for management. They refused to listen to him at the time, so instead he was invited by Japanese business leaders to share his wisdom with them. After applying these significant components, he largely assisted in shaping Japanese business methods into what they are today – innovation moguls.

A few of Deming's outlined principles are as follows:

Cease dependence on inspection to achieve quality. Eliminate the need for inspection on a mass basis by building quality into the product in the first place.

Improve constantly and forever the system of production and service, to improve quality and productivity, and thus constantly decrease costs.

Break down barriers between departments. People in research, design, sales, and production must work as a team, to foresee problems of production and in use that may be encountered with the product or service.

Leaders will not be able to expand beyond their current limits and see issues from multiple points of view without making the effort to dip their toes in first. To culturally expand their awareness, both in the company and in the world, they must adopt practices that encourage their education. Increase your network and begin establishing healthy relationships with the heads of other departments. As a leader of design for example, you will gain valuable insights by speaking with a leader in the sales department to know what specifically people are responding to and what they are not.

If you are working in an international company or even if you are not, speaking with employees of a similar sector from a different cultural background will provide a different way of thinking. A Japanese technician will think differently than a Californian one, and thus may be able to provide a solution where the other sees an obstacle. Travel and reading up on translated business articles will also assist in developing these alternative perspectives.

By focusing on the larger picture we can see what results as an effect of our direct efforts. Then by zooming in further to analyze individual components more closely, we can see how each department relates to another. We begin to understand the intricate relationships of complex business systems and better hone in on what went wrong and where, when it occurs. This further aids in our process of developing a solution because we will have gained insight as to how each department's decisions is affected by the other. That way, we can optimally come up with a solution that will benefit all departments and prevent future snags in the system as a whole. The system is intricate, and we must understand and respect it in that way to successfully work as a team.

If there is a problem, a good leader must be able to figure out the root of the issue, and analyze the proper business processes in order to fix it. The solution to a problem must be such that it leaves no scope for harm to the company a few years down the line. Looking for quick fixes are sometimes the biggest reasons why leaders fail their position.

One other crucial aspect to take into account is the ambiguity of the business world. Because of globalization and the intricacies of business systems in supply and communication that were mentioned before, it is impossible to know everything that is going on and all the factors that add in. In that way, you must develop an attitude cavalier enough to not be too swayed by constant change where quick decisions must be made. It becomes a matter of considering all the available data, drawing upon a multitude of various resources including perspectives and people, trusting your gut instinct that comes with experience and allowing your better intuition to take over at times.

Consistency

In homage of this quality, consistency needs to be spread across the board, evident in everything a leader does. From punctuality, prioritizing, communication and feedback to emotional stability, integrity, ethics, empathy and assertiveness, consistency is a major asset to build strength, confidence and trust in yourself and those you are leading.

In order to stay on top of things and to show to your team a sense of faith and reliability, a leader should almost always be the first person to arrive to work. It conveys preparedness and a jump ahead in the game that is crucial for competitively innovative markets. It will also provide you the time to get set up for the day so that you may make yourself more available to your team members later on who may have questions and need guidance. It should almost be implicit then that the leader is the last to leave. Hardly micromanaging, it is simply wise for a leader to make sure that at the end of the day, they know where their employees and their company stands.

Prioritizing tasks is the only way to stay organized and focused so that you and your team members can do what they need to get done. There will always be a list of things to do, and on the rare occasions when you or your team members may actually finish the expectations in that time period with room left to spare, there is still plenty of research and planning to do to keep your business moving forward. Keep lists and progress charts up to date and make a habit of knowing what needs to be taken care of next so you are not caught off-guard. And then, make sure that your employees are aware of the same. This will ensure a greater sense of confidence in them because if they know that their leader is staying on top of things, they will be more motivated to do so as well without having to stress.

Communication, communication, communication. It's becoming a theme, isn't it? And it can't be emphasized enough. Your employees need to know how they are doing at their job. They need to know the results of their work so that they can provide feedback. They need to be able to know that they can come to you if they have a work-related issue or an idea to be able to point something out that perhaps you were unaware of or had overlooked. You should be able to provide consistent encouragement for team members' commendable efforts, constructive criticism or corrections to mistakes or low-quality production on a consistent basis, and regulated updates for your team on how the business is doing directly from source.

Consistency of integrity and ethics means that for the business or group venture, no matter what obstacles you face you must always, always stick to your established values without exception. No cutting corners. If you begin to cut corners outside of the business, you will eventually notice the same short-handed practice from your employees within the business. Monkey see, monkey do. Be the upstanding example. It also means that you treat your employees fairly and consistently. If you choose to deny a certain privilege to one employee, do it across the board. It is your decision, but at least you will be consistent. Making exceptions or favoring one employee over another will attract disharmony and tension in the workplace.

Be steady in your assertiveness for the same reasons. You can present yourself in a friendly manner and still maintain an authoritative approach. If you let up because you don't feel like dealing with confrontation that day, you are giving your power over to that employee and they won't respect you for it, and then it will catch on throughout the workplace. It is the idea that if you give them an inch, they make take a mile, so avoid giving that opportunity the chance. You hold the cards. Be fair, make sure that you deal out your authority evenly.

A consistent approach needs to be followed by a leader in order to ensure that the workers are motivated to act to their full potential. This is achieved by adopting various systematic processes such as delegation, fixing deadlines and providing feedback.

Motivation

The main purpose of a leader is to influence and motivate people. A good leader is one who sets an example for his or her team and acts like a role model and guide for them in times of need. Strategies for effective leadership are discussed in the upcoming chapter, but what you need to know now is that one of the most desired qualities and prerequisites of being a leader is the ability to motivate people. In many ways, a leader is a visionary, and thus it is vital that they are able to convince the people of the goal they need to fulfill.

Prepare yourself before going into a meeting or when planning to speak with a specific employee. This will help you focus on what you expect from your team rather than what they are not doing right. You want to avoid putting others on the defensive. By precisely vocalizing what you are looking for, you will give a clear understanding for your employees to receive. By focusing on what you expect from them, you are inherently cultivating a more positive approach and avoiding traps like blaming or lowering others' self-esteem.

Get people to think about their actions that they possibly haven't even considered by asking them 'why' questions. You must first be able to identify an issue specifically and then approach it objectively as an observation without making accusations. For example, ask, "Why do you think your number of sales has dropped this month?" Be genuine when asking. This shows empathy which will help your employee open up. Wouldn't you really want to know what's causing them to perform this way anyways? Once you get them to talk about it, turn the conversation into focusing on solutions.

Tactics like asking solution-oriented questions are good motivators for discouraged employees because it puts power in their hands that they can work with. Allowing employees to come up with their own solutions gives them more space to manage themselves, providing them room to grow. When speaking with your team members, formulate your questions in an open-ended way that also directs them to come to a solution that you both can agree on.

Allow team members as much freedom to complete a set of clearly defined goals in the way that they want as possible. As long as you can be explicit with your expectations, giving team members leniency to tackle the job in their own way will keep them happy and help garner their loyalty to your company rather than a competitor's.

Permit casual dress at work for those who are not meeting with clients in person. Provide flexible work hours so the family people can attend their children's events or those who wish to hit the gym in the morning or sleep in just a little longer can do so. You might be surprised at just what a difference allowing people to be themselves in this way makes a difference for their emotional wellbeing (which equals better performance at work) and sense of motivation.

Responsibility

People who assume responsibility and do not shy from it make for good leaders. A diligent leader is never afraid to accept extra responsibilities that other may not be willing to accept. However, responsibility often times is a double-edged sword that can fall back on the one wielding it if they are not prepared to handle it correctly.

Let's talk power. As a leader, when you hear that word – power – it initiates some enthusiasm within you. Why else would you vie for a leadership position, right? It provides you the ability to realize big goals, to usher about change in the world, and it puts you in the driver's seat to control to an extent what direction that change takes the rest of us. Some part of you, no matter how big or miniscule, is attracted to power. And so the question comes, when you search within yourself: what exactly drives your desire for that power, and how will you use it?

For the most part, power does not make one responsible. Responsibility is a composition of both innate and learned qualities within a person that we have discussed throughout this book, such as good communication skills, listening skills, consistency, the ability to self-motivate, integrity, focus, and diligence. Power often illuminates these already-contained qualities or exposes the lack of them.

Even with high standards and polished integrity, leaders can and do fall short when it comes to exerting power effectively and responsibly. It can become too much and get to people's heads. In 1959, psychologists John French and Bertram Raven developed a structure for understanding different types of power and in her book, *What Keeps Leaders up at Night*, Nicole Lipkin elucidates why it's important for leaders to know what type of power they are using. Knowing what type of power you wield will help you better manage it when dealing with people as well as focus on the more sustaining ones that provide affluent promise.

Legitimate power is the one we may most often think of earning through promotions and initiative: it is when someone attains a high position, gaining control over others. It's important to know with this power that it was given and it can be taken away, even from founders, so it should not be abused. The pivot on which this power resides mostly has to do with the favor of the employees. If they trust you with it, they will approve when you exert your legitimate power. However if you have risen to a position of power and your employees do not feel that you deserve it, that can affect the whole company negatively.

Coercive power – power lead by fear and a certain kind of muscling – should never be used. It will be a short-term power because you will lose respect and loyalty from your employees. No one will want to work with you.

Expert power comes from the experience and fine skills you have honed over the years, in association with reputable evidence of knowledge accumulated in education, most often in the form of a Masters or Doctorate degree. In essence, you're smart, you know it, and you know how to apply it. More importantly, people will pay you for it and will be willing to work with you or under you to continue supplying you with this power. No one can take this power away from you. The responsibility lies in the need to continue learning and improving yourself so that you may stay on top of your game and continue leading effectively.

Informational power is short-term. It does not necessarily build credit to your reputation or encourage influence over others. It is the kind where once the information is shared, the power goes with it. We live in the information age. Competition sets businesses apart by weeks, so this kind of power does not last for long, and should not be considered for a long-term strategy.

The power of reward is found among those who are able to motivate people to perform in order to win raises, promotions and awards. According to Lipkin, people who administer performance reviews that determine raises and bonuses wield a certain amount of reward power. They influence others to be more productive and effective in their jobs, which becomes a win for the company at large.

Connection power can be directly associated to networking. If you can develop the skills to create and maintain professional relationships with those in power, then you stand to be influential yourself. Building important partnerships with influential people puts you in a position to connect others with your network, which lends a great power to you. The responsibility here means that you must be able to appropriately judge the character of the people that you are linking into your network, because once you recommend them, their actions become a reflection upon you.

Referent power is affiliated with the esteemed qualities and traits that were mentioned early on in this section – honesty, good communication, integrity, and so on. It is considered to be the most important and real power that leaders should embrace. It hinges on the development of quality relationships built with colleagues. The power here is derived from people who admire and respect you, so your upstanding qualities become a direct influence upon them. You become the good leader by example, and can use this power to begin directing the course of action for your associates who rely on you.

The next time you think about that word, keep in mind that with great power comes great responsibility.

No bias

A good leader is expected to be completely unbiased. Leaders who show bias in the workspace create a disparity between workers, which leads to a noxious work environment. Such behaviour is unhealthy for the smooth running of the business. A leader should also avoid their personal equation with a fellow worker that may cloud their judgment and decision making in their favour.

This means taking cautious entrustment of the incentives that you provide to your team members, making sure that the origin of your desire to provide these incentives comes from a business standpoint and not a personal one.

Why is the phrase, “It’s not personal, it’s business,” so commonly heard? Even though it is taken out of context sometimes, this expression reiterates purpose of action in the workplace. Sometimes the managerial decisions that have to be made as leaders are very difficult ones. Leaders must value their employees and realize that it is successful employees that make a company successful, however the leader must ultimately do what is good for the business. This means giving a promotion to the right person for the job and not to someone just because you are on friendlier terms with them.

Even though personality and work performance may be intertwined, a leader’s conduct with employees must always lean toward work performance. You may find certain aspects of an employee’s personality irritating for example, but it would be erroneous to criticize them unless it was directly affecting their work, other people’s work around them, or violating certain ethics of the company. And it would be a waste of time on the leader’s part to try to make the facts fit the theory.

A good leader must practice emotional stability and separate their personal judgements from their professional ones in the company, seeing everyone objectively to guarantee fairness.

Self-Assessment

Good leaders are consistently taking stock of their shortcomings and personal strengths. They like to question their strengths and weaknesses, in order to always stay on top of the game. They choose to categorize their abilities and their shortcomings in order to assign tasks to their workforce better by evaluating the strengths of the employees and deciding who would be perfect for the job.

Good leaders do not rush recruitment, and hire people who complement their skills. Meanwhile, they work on their weaknesses to become better workers and more productive to the workspace. Working on their weaknesses also provides the opportunity to see the world around them from a different standpoint, which opens to door to more insightful opportunities. They remove the ego from their perspective so they can see their actions and though processes and others' with an objective lens.

This type of vision helps leaders also bring a sense of honesty to the workplace that may seem uncomfortable to share at first, however as workers see the leader applying the same principles to themselves, they will gain incentive to be more open to this ongoing process.

The more objective a leader can be with themselves, the more that they can do so with others and by nature show others how to do it for themselves. It goes to show that focusing on weaknesses is not a horrible or cruel thing because it offers gifts of potential, growth, and brings a shared sense of humanity to those who are open to it. Team members and their leader can then better support each other, knowing directly where to apply that support. This in turn will enforce a sense of togetherness that will help build the strength of the team as a whole.

Introduction to the Enneagram

The Enneagram (pronounced: ANY-uh-gram) is a prolific symbol of ancient alchemy (the science of transformation) that is over 5,000 years old, although its exact origins remain unknown. While its application has been attributed to many spiritual practices, the Enneagram, "ennea" meaning nine, has provided a very lucrative and practical use in the business world.

The Enneagram illustrates nine different personality types that together comprise a single unit, and has been used worldwide to assist business managers and leaders in forming optimal work teams for collaborative efforts and project execution. It has helped assess which employees are the best in working together and determine which employees are best for the job in working on specific projects.

The nine personality types and brief descriptions of each are as follows:

1 – The Reformer: Perfectionists, responsible, fixated on improvement

2 – The Helper (Mentor): Selfless, socially aware, extroverted

3 – The Achiever: Hard working, competitive, focused on the presentation of success

4 – The Individualist (Designer): Identity-conscious, unique, individualistic

5 – The Investigator: Thorough, perceptive, proactive

6 – The Loyalist (Troubleshooter): Engaging, diligent, likable

7 – The Enthusiast: Creative, future oriented, open minded

8 – The Challenger: Self-confident, decisive, practical

9 – The Peacemaker: Harmonic, accommodating, reassuring

What is unique about the Enneagram is that it recognizes the spectrum of personal qualities, from the basic characteristics of each personality type, to when each type is at their best and when they are unhealthy as well, affected by factors such as prolonged stress. In this way, one can use this system to help identify their own strengths and weaknesses as well as others'.

A good leader would be able to make great use of this tool not only to identify their own shortcomings and work on improving them, but efficiently delegate tasks and workloads to the right people. As a leader should always be seeking out ways to boost morale and help improve their workers' individual skills, one can apply the knowledge of the Enneagram to assign certain jobs to team members that will stimulate their growth.

Chapter 3

Strategies for Leading in Business

To progress in business, you need to possess the eye for identifying a potential opportunity and capitalizing on it. A good leader possesses the skill set to turn the smallest of opportunities into something big that benefits the company. The strategies and skills discussed in this section of the book will help you navigate the unknown and challenge yourself to take high risks and make smart corporate decisions.

The Enneagram in practice

There are several books written on the application of the Enneagram in business settings such as *Bringing Out the Best in Yourself at Work* and *What Type of Leader Are You?* By Ginger Lapid-Bogda, PhD. There are also Enneagram assessment tests that you can take and/or have your team members take. One free test can be found at

www.eclecticenergies.com/enneagram/test.php.

Authors Riso and Hudson are leading authorities in this sector that have spent years accumulating scientifically-proven research and developing it into what they call the Riso-Hudson Enneagram Type Indicator (RHETI). This forced-choice personality test of 144 paired statements is backed by The Enneagram Institute and is designed as a scientifically valid assertion for professional use in business that may be sampled and purchased through The Enneagram Institute's website. They also provide a booklet that goes into great depth describing each of the nine Enneagram personality types.

Developing awareness of the nine personality types of the Enneagram and one's own personality type eventually leads to intimate self-discovery and professional development. This helps enhance your own growth as a leader by knowing yourself and how to better conduct yourself, and knowing those working under you and how to best approach them in the workplace. It also aids in delegating the proper tasks to the appropriate individuals of your team, and assembling the best crack team to take on a particular project while collectively driving toward future successes.

As a prime example, employing a type 8 (the challenger) will provide vision and confidence, type 9 (the peacemaker) will assist in bringing people together and listening to their needs, a type 1 (the reformer) will maintain quality control and the ethical standards you have established, 2's (the mentor) make excellent HR representatives to serve people and anticipate their needs, a 3 (the achiever) may head up the promotional and communication skills of the job, 4's (the designer) can provide product design and intuition to the impact of the product on customers and affiliates, a 5 type (the investigator) would initiate innovation and contribute technical expertise, type 6 (the troubleshooter) would make a great regulator of feedback and teamwork, and 7's (the enthusiast) can provide the energy and optimism necessary to keep the team motivated and moving forward.

As leaders, we must be able to recognize that different people need to be managed differently because depending on the personality type, people will respond to different kinds of stimuli. By using the details of the Enneagram types to one's advantage, a leader can identify a certain personality type's habits and train of thought so that they can approach that person and motivate them more effectively.

The leader who employs these principles will develop an understanding of how to speak other's languages, which are often very diverse, and then it will become easier to deal with conflicts more fairly. Not only that, by speaking another's language, a leader will be able to get their objectives across more clearly and check concepts with their team members more concisely.

The Enneagram in effect helps to diversify a leader's perspective so that they understand nine different ways to solve a problem at all times. They can better reflect the values they set forth to increase job satisfaction and productivity. With training and practice in understanding the Enneagram, a leader can coach their team members to work at their highest capabilities by developing the insights into what motivates them. This takes the guesswork out of team assembly and saves invaluable time in greasing the wheels for employees to work together synergistically.

Question the status quo

Smart leaders are always challenging notions, roles and the thinking styles of people around them. Strategic leaders challenge the assumptions and expectations set by other people, encouraging diverse opinions and ideas. If you want to be a good leader, do not be afraid to contest people and their ideas.

This requires an open mind, boldness and patience, which we discussed before as being the qualities required in a leader. Strategic leaders take action after careful consideration of all their options, from different viewpoints, and this comes only after challenging the status quo.

This is assuredly one of the top characteristics of successful entrepreneurs. Great leaders must question the set standard. More importantly, they must have the energy to reimagine their own approach to tasks and consistently reinvent themselves to keep an edge ahead of competition. By maintaining this attitude as a leader, you will encourage your workers to do the same so that it becomes a mindset adopted for the entire organization. Creating this imprint at the core of your organization will keep it running autonomously and well into the future. Sometimes it so happens that a person has a selective approach to tackling a problem that makes them predictable, and in the long run, inefficient. A fresh outlook is very important when dealing with problems, as not all the problems are the same and can be solved in the same way. Well-thought out solutions may sometimes prove impractical because insufficient insight is gathered from the people around the one who is providing the solution.

How to induce the ability to challenge?

- Compile a diverse group of people, and ask them about the long-standing assumptions of your business. See what they come up with; integrate them into your future policies.

- Conduct meetings where open dialogue and conflict are encouraged. Microsoft and Dell are two companies noted for their atmosphere of independently-minded people that are encouraged for their dissimilar points of view to help drive innovation forward. The idea is that perpetuating this creative dialogue will free you as the leader to further focus on pushing the applications of your intellect.

- Come up with a rotating position to keep the status quo interesting and create a challenge among the workers. This has been proven to effectively motivate employees to keep from getting bored at their positions and reduce turnover rates. It is a strategy that fits the pace of the business world today which combines company loyalty with job diversification and improvement of workers' understanding of infrastructure, which serves to advance proficiency.

- Consult third parties not involved directly in the decision making or its outcome to get an unbiased and smart perspective on the consequences and nuances of a decision.

Think ahead

Lapses in judgment are often the result of the inability to detect threats or opportunities in business. The market is always evolving, and so are the needs of consumers. It is necessary to be up to date with current trends in order to maximize profit. In order for this to happen, a leader needs to identify opportunities well in advance so he/she can assign duties and come up with a strategy well ahead of time.

Cultivate genuine curiosity in your company's practices and policies, as well as that of your competitors and your business industry as a whole. A funny thing happens when you develop curiosity about a particular subject – a kind of magnetic attraction grows where you are able to draw your attention to multiple values of a particular domain and on top of that, you find yourself enjoying the process, which fuels it even more.

In alignment with curiosity of your business environment, continue to work in expanding your knowledge and experience. You will inevitably being making relevant associations and seeing patterns across supposedly unrelated fields. Broaden yourself, be flexible, and you will be able to identify the opportunities within challenges to turn your company around.

A good leader may be great at dealing with crises, sure. But sometimes they fail to recognize the weak signals both inside and outside the organization. It is necessary to diversify in order to meet demands. Cultivate the ability to anticipate. This can be done by taking into account the perspective of the competitors, consumers and the workers alike.

How can you improve the ability to anticipate?

- Evaluate the performance of your rivals; examine the actions they have taken which baffle you and the ones that have paid off.

- Visualize different scenarios vividly, imagine future prospects and try to plan a course of action accordingly.

- Interact with consumers, suppliers and business partners to get some perspective on the challenges they might be facing.

- Make it a point to visit conventions, conferences and events to get an idea of the booming market trends and practices.

- Conduct market surveys and researches.

Improve your ability to interpret

The best leaders are the ones who are able to interpret well. Challenging situations around one will lead to complex situations and complex information. As a good leader, you must be able to interpret the input you have received and seek the right insights.

Strategic thinking, while commonly practiced as an isolated event only a couple times out of the year, should be a skill that is used on a daily basis. This is the number one difference that separates highly effective leaders from the rest. Therefore as a daily practice, it becomes a frame of mind rather than just a slew of methods. This is why it is such a particularly difficult leadership quality to master if it doesn't come naturally, but with practice and endurance this too can set you and your company leagues apart from competitors. A good leader is able to recognize patterns, identify hidden implications, eliminate ambiguity and approach the situation with a sharp analytical outlook. What good are surveys and researches performed on the market, and observations of the consumers if you are unable to interpret the data and act accordingly? A good leader is expected to be able to connect the dots and come up with a strategy.

How to interpret better?

- Try to list at least two to three explanations for any ambiguous data that you are supposed to analyze. Create mock templates of this data and share it with uninvolved colleagues. Compare relevance of your explanations with theirs, aiming to derive any further insights from alternative justifications they come up with.

- Ask for perspectives from stakeholders and unbiased parties. Developing a mental library of relevant information in your business will expand your thinking beyond your current position and daily tasks.

- Consider assigning a mentor or hiring a strategic consultant to train under, whether it be for you, fellow managers, or top employees.

- Catalogue any missing information and form a conclusive basis for your hypothesis. Do this on a regular basis and set aside time to practice strategic planning by yourself and in meetings with others

- Alternate between zooming in on the details and out, in order to see the big picture.

- Take breaks, clear your head and Meditate for 10 to 15 minutes, focusing on deep breathing. It brings oxygen to the brain which nourishes your cells and encourages clearer inner vision. Then think again. Do not burn yourself out.

Pace yourself

Among people, data, strategies, mind frame shaping and policies to manage, the demands of leadership can be overwhelming at times. Keeping up with market trends and groundbreaking innovations can leave you feeling swamped or swept away if you are not able to effectively pace yourself.

Consider your tactical footing: you always want to be moving if you are going to make any finite headway for your personal and company goals, so you must maintain a light touch that exerts adaptability, quick decision making, fast redirection of focus when necessary and so on. At the same time, your efforts need to be well planned out and effective enough to make an impression that will carry you through for the long-term, along with your whole company and all the people you are managing.

Such circumstances dictate you to be operating at your absolute best so that you may encourage your subordinates to do the same as well. For this, you need to know yourself well. You must know what you are capable of, how far you can push yourself while still remaining effectual and what habits to practice that ensure a mental, emotional and physical well-being.

How to pace yourself effectively?

- Stay highly organized with a system that works best for you, so that you get the full scope of where you've been, where you currently are, and where you plan on heading at all times. This can take shape in a combination of schedules, color-coded charts, to-do lists, mind maps, task-oriented applications like OneNote and so on.

- To reiterate, because it is often overlooked or ruled out: take breaks! The brain is a processor, and making it run consistently throughout the day will cause it to overheat and run slower. You think you are doing well now? Are you reaching for coffee or an energy drink? Take short breaks – 10 to 15 minutes – throughout the day to refresh your body and your way of thinking.

- Meditate daily, whenever you get the chance. Take a few moments to tune your mind out of tasking long enough to come back into a sense of calm and inner strength. When you can de-stress and reassure yourself of your power with feeling, you can get back to doing the quality work for which you know you are capable.

- Be highly conscious of time management. Fill your day with priorities and activities that are most important to you and synchronize them with your company goals. Consider where you could tighten up lost time and redirect it into one or a few of those valuable activities.

Find common ground

Strong, strategic leaders do not allow scope for huge conflict among parties that are both involved in the same organizational policy. Here, what works best is finding common ground to unite stakeholders with varying agendas and conflicting views.

Negotiating and influencing people are the foundation to becoming a good leader. A good leader is expected to build trust and have an active outreach. With the onset of globalization and diversity in workforce, alienation may arise between sectors of the organization. Regular meetings and increased interaction are important when dealing with fellow leaders in order to overcome hurdles.

People want to enjoy their work and connect with their colleagues. Most people have simply not had enough experience in stimulating positive social engagement or just do not know how to go about it inclusively. When people enjoy their work, they develop more creative solutions to problems, feel less stressed, and generally become more efficient and productive. Focus on creating an atmosphere that your team members can look forward to everyday.

How to improve your ability to align?

- Avoid complaints of not knowing by communicating early with employees and making them aware of the tasks at hand. Be specific. Outline objectives in many different forms, such as verbal communication, emails, written reports and so on.

- Identify areas of conflicts and resistance and incorporate them into conversations to expose them. Do your best to be straightforward without placing blame. Focus on the importance of clearing the issue itself rather than trying to pin the source of it. Many rumors and office tiffs grow into problematic distractions because they find their power in the background and whispers. Once they are brought to the forefront so that everyone is aware, that power is lost.

- Monitor the positions of stakeholders carefully during the implementation of your strategy.

- Look for coalitions and hidden agendas and then map the positions of external stakeholders on your initiative.

- Reward the workers who offer their support to team alignment. Give them opportunities to lead teams for small venture projects or assist in organizing group events where possible. Workers appreciate experiences that allow them to boost their skills.

- Strategically plan team-building exercises on a regular basis to enhance employee cohesiveness. First identify the purpose of the exercise – if your effort is just a good idea without any real planning involved, it can backfire on you – do you want to increase communication between your employees? Boost morale? Establish trust? Then fit an appropriate exercise to your desired purpose.

Neuro Linguistic Programming (NLP)

Successful leaders are frequently on the lookout for ways to improve themselves and be more effective in getting things done. As the working world grows and we extend our outreach into vast global networks, the need to be more impressionable rises. Our ability to speak to others' interests in order to gain closer relationships demands new skill sets that help to refine our approach.

As people learn more about each other, indeed, as we learn more about ourselves and how our brains operate, we begin to delve into the subtleties that cause a greater impact and bring about more significant change in how we see the world and what we are capable of doing within it. The most important aspect of this change as we evolve is to see it as a behavioural shift rather than an intellectual skill to be acquired.

How to encourage easier, faster connections?

- Look into programs that offer NLP training workshops for businesses that you and your teammates may attend. Research the benefits and make a proposal to your superiors to get company funding for the event.

- Understand that everyone's successes and failures are based upon the way we see the world. Our perceptions define our reality. This is why the core principle of so many motivational seminars is to think positively and make those positive thoughts as much of a reality with daily affirmations and vision boards as possible until they actually manifest.

- Respect others' viewpoints. The sooner you understand that we all think differently, the faster and more capable you will become in communicating with others on a higher level of quality. You will eliminate assumptions of what others mean by developing a keener interpretation of multiple viewpoints.

- By all means, be adaptable. Trying the same thing and expecting a different result is a good way to turn Einstein in his grave. Flexibility opens doors to stronger relationships and increased influence. It also lubricates the learning process by taking a different approach to previous mistakes and alters the thought patterns that keep us repeating the same results, like, 'People don't understand what we're trying to do here.'

Make efficient decisions

In times of turmoil and uncertainty, it falls on the shoulders of those in authoritative positions to make the tough calls and make decisions even without sufficient information, and do so fast. Even in such a situation, smart leaders are expected to carefully weigh their options without getting locked into making go/no-go decisions. Leaders are expected to have faith in their convictions and take both short and long-term goals into account even when forced to make a decision quickly.

Try to approach situations in a methodical way, do not limit yourself to yes/no proposition. A good leader doesn't let him or herself get cornered into making a choice without being offered the alternative to come up with their own solution.

How to improve your ability to decide?

- Include your team in the decision-making process. Ask them about other possible options.

- Split big decisions into smaller components and aim to understand unintended repercussions better.

- Evaluate the team you want to be directly involved with the decision making, based on how you think they may influence the success of your decision. This is another area where implementing the use of the Enneagram would be highly effective. Considering the nature of the problem and the specific topics involved, you can determine which personality types would be best suited to handle the situation.

- Experiment, instead of playing big bets in a haste. The best counteraction for unexpected circumstances or foreign territory is to be prepared. It sounds contradictory – how can one be prepared for something unexpected? Look to business forecasts. Stick to your team's core strengths. Allow experimental side projects for your most efficient team members before surprises occur to fan out your options for when they do.

Chapter 4

Business Coaching

Leadership is not just about influencing people and negotiating with them; leadership involves building a taskforce that is motivated and skilled enough to tackle the work at hand. The ability to coach has made its way to one of the added qualities of a good leader. Nowadays, workplaces operate on the belief that the workers need to develop simultaneously. Few managers can make coaching work. Coaching aims at helping people learn how to grow, rather than giving directions.

While coaching their subordinates, leaders must keep in mind the following aims:

Building trust

Coaches must have a lot of patience, establish boundaries and invoke trust in their subordinates and fellow workers.

The concept of trust in the workplace is somewhat of a tricky one. It may appear straightforward and simple to some, but it should not be taken for granted. It may seem to be too much effort to be worth the time or simply frivolous for others, although the effects of established trust among employees in the workplace have proven to provide boundless prestige for the company as a whole.

Way back when business and industry first found their footholds within society and began developing legitimate, long-standing reputations, up until about the mid-90s, organizations felt they had the upper hand when it came to maintaining employee loyalty. Often times that's simply the way it was – employees would compete for jobs within a company and spend the rest of their working days in hopes of climbing up the ladder and earning a pension upon retirement. Their success and job security was dependent upon remaining loyal to their company, whether they agreed with the company's values or not. Transferring from one company to another in those days often meant either starting in a lower position or working to earn their superiors' trust all over again for years on end.

The game has changed quite a bit since then, right around the turn of the century. Now it is the companies competing for employee loyalty for many reasons. Companies face a frequent consideration to either hire new managers from outside the company or promote from within. Employees have a greater flexibility to choose in honing their skills with one organization or packing up shop and moving to another that will better suit their needs, whether that may mean a greater potential for promotion, better pay, more lucrative perks, or a friendlier company culture.

Now the responsibility of establishing trust within a company falls on the leaders and coaches within the various levels of that company's infrastructure. Leaders are called to become excellent representatives of their organization's values and mission as well as that of their specific branch, themselves as their own word, promises, and actions, and the affiliates under their direction. The must take it upon themselves to make sure that everyone in their guidance system is working cooperatively and focused as a whole toward the bigger picture. And the way they may succinctly achieve that is by building trust in the workplace, beginning individually.

The key components to building trust with your employees have actually already been outlined throughout this book, so they will be outlined here again and if you should need a more in-depth refresher, you can refer back to those specific sections.

What does it take to build trust?

Good communication skills – Be precise and to the point, explicitly outline your expectations and cover any ambiguous areas. Check for understanding among your employees with questions that elicit specific, detailed responses.

Good listening skills – Look deeper into your employees' verbal expressions for what they really mean and what they are not saying as well. Look for words that describe feelings. Develop a keen sense of what their facial expressions and body language is telling you that their words are not, and then acknowledge it aloud with them. Repeat back what they share with you to show your understanding and correct any misinterpretations.

Being open – Employees will have a difficult time trusting you if they can't even reach you. Make your employees aware that you are available to them. Practice patience with them instead of being short. Your work priorities are important of course, however the employees you manage collectively make a greater contribution to the company, and in a leadership position their performance is ultimately your number one priority.

Being consistent – The more consistent you are in your actions, your words, and following through with your promises through good times and hard times, the more you convey to your subordinates that you are reliable. When they know for themselves that you are reliable, they will be more apt to place their trust in you.

Motivate! – Motivation is like food for the soul. The person who is able to effectively arouse inspiration within another will be remembered and respected for a long time. This is an invaluable asset for you to develop as a leader, so get to know your employees and what drives them, then find creative ways to stimulate that drive and provide opportunities for your employees to exercise it.

One brief caution when dealing with trust in the workplace is that you do not want your employees to come running to you every time they have a problem or be divulging information that is too personal or practice conduct that goes beyond professional boundaries. It is a common phenomenon known as transference that when people recognize a person as powerful and place their trust in them, they may lose their sense of what is appropriate in the professional relationship. Be firm in establishing boundaries. Practice your assertiveness to your employees by letting them know that while you are open and available to them, you are in a professional workplace and your relationship must remain as such.

Provide assessment

Regular feedback lets people be in the know-how regarding their performance, and provides them with self-awareness.

You'll want to make sure that every assessment you make with your employees is geared toward their improvement. So then, do you think that blunt criticism is going to make a productive imprint on an employee's performance? Perhaps, actually, it just might. As a coach of many different kinds of people, you cannot apply a one-size-fits-all approach to every person. Some managers do this, and while they may achieve some results, they are meager at best. Your goal should be to optimize each of your employees' potentials. In order to do that, you must treat them as individuals and understand to which style of appraisal they best respond. Understanding the psychology of the Enneagram can help do this.

For those who are direct, no-nonsense types of people that like to work hard, blunt criticism may just be the appropriate thing to spur them on. The fact is that you can address these people in a straightforward manner for the most part because you will be speaking their language, and they will appreciate that. On the other hand for those types of people who are more sensitive or are constantly seeking approval for their work, a sympathetic and thoughtful approach in turn will help get your message across more resolutely. You need to take an active role in getting a feel for how each of your employees respond best.

For longer term reviews you can practice techniques like the compliment sandwich. This involves highlighting positive qualities of your worker's performance at both the beginning and end of the assessment. It provides encouragement and a buffer for serious adjustments or improvements that need to be made, which you can address in the middle of your review. The worker will walk away with a level perspective of their strong and weak points, and they will be more confident in rectifying those areas that they need to work on.

Remember that like anything that needs maintenance and supervision, your workers need feedback and monitored in their progress on a regular basis. Waiting until performance reviews at the end of the year will not cover all the small changes that could really help your employees progress week to week. Do not wait. Make it a weekly practice, but make sure that the material you submit to your workers is of quality. If there is nothing in particular that you can think of for them to improve, give praise for specific things they did well or suggest that now is the time they can work on pushing themselves beyond their limits into new territory.

Keep your employees informed of their performance on a regular basis and they will be better able to gauge their progress by themselves over time. You will be instilling an important value of self-assessment that will help add to the scope of the employees' purpose in the company and how their work makes an exact contribution to the company as a whole.

Support and encourage

Coaches are expected to be good listeners, and allow workers to vent without judging them harshly. Employees are encouraged to reach towards their goals.

When it comes to good listening skills, it's not just about hearing what others say, it's about hearing what they *don't* say and what they actually *mean*. This can be extremely difficult since we all interpret information differently, even the same information, and we all have a tendency to assume we know what another person is talking about when we are really only seeing it from one point of view – our own.

The first step towards being able to support and encourage others is to take your own ego out of the picture. This means adopting an unassuming, open-minded approach toward people to achieve the most desirable outcome. Often times this also means achieving the desired mutual understanding of a conversation by addressing the other person's concerns first before even bringing up the actual issue. And sometimes after taking this different approach, the situation resolves itself without even having to address the issue.

How does one do this? The answer is simple – listening. The practice is difficult only because it requires us to unlearn the way we have been taught to get what we want for the good of the big picture and take a different approach altogether. But we can learn this too. It starts with practicing to slow the mind-wandering down and place our full attention on what the person in front of us is saying.

We are used to being barraged with information and priorities in and out of the workplace so much that it can become overwhelming for our minds to processes. Meditation helps, which is essentially the practice of focusing our attention onto a single point of reality and thereby slowing all other extraneous thoughts down. It elicits mental peace and clarity, which are necessary for good listening.

Stop interrupting. It requires practice and patience, but try not to complete another's sentence for them. We often desire to share an understanding in what others are saying so readily that we make the mistake of assuming what the other person is thinking. More often than not, we assume incorrectly.

We also have the tendency to get caught up in the choice of language another uses where a little voice in our head will raise a red flag and judge, "This person's grammar is awful," or, "That word is not at all what I would use to describe that." Perhaps the word you would use could describe the situation in another way, but both meanings would still be relevant. Turn off the voice in your head and allow the other person to complete their train of thought so you get the best possible picture of what they are trying to relate.

The most successful people are those who are able to relate in some way to the people around them. If you make an effort to understand why another person feels the way he or she does, you will gain the referent power based on trustworthiness that Nicole Lipkin ascribes. The person will feel that they have been heard, and they will be more willing to comply with your instructions. Pay attention to subtleties of words that express feelings or needs and body language as well to gain a deeper understanding of how a person actually feels.

Paraphrase what you've heard back to the person to check for accuracy and understanding. Expand upon what you heard the person share from both verbal and nonverbal cues, including emotions, and acknowledge this aloud to the person to confirm your understanding. Do your best not to be critical; judgements are only steps backwards and lose ground with those you are trying to engage. Be honest with how you feel yourself and tell the person what you think after acknowledging what they've said.

Listening requires a great deal of effort, although the rewards pay off big in the long run because you will have a team full of people who trust in you and understand that their needs and your needs are being met.

Challenge their thinking

Coaches are expected to ask open-ended questions, invoke a thinking process for alternative solutions, and motivate risk taking within reasonable bounds.

Open-ended questions are the kinds that go beyond stimulating a simple "yes" or "no" answer. "Yes" and "no," while perhaps answering your question directly, don't really tell you much except that perhaps you should be asking better questions. To get the most information out of your employees, to get a sense of how they personally feel and what specifically can be encouraged or improved, you need to ask the kind of open-ended questions that stimulate discussion. These will provide deeper insights for you and your team and give you all something more pliable with which to work.

So instead of asking "Were you happy with the results you got?" try, "Why do you think you got results you did?" Most open-ended questions will begin with "What," "How," "Why," or "Describe to me..." You will find that close-ended questions often make an assumption or implication in their wording that become traps for employees and stifle their genuine thoughts. A few examples are, "Do you think the reports reflect our best productivity?" and "Others are telling me you have been falling short on your quota. Do you agree?" Open-ended questioning should stimulate an employee to think critically as well as generate opportunities for them or the company to move forward positively.

The company Google provides a unique example of how to stimulate their employees' thinking and motivate risk-taking within reasonable bounds. The innovation department of this multibillion dollar company recognizes passion, one of the four cornerstones of successful leadership, as a bigger motivator than money. Eric Schmidt, a founder of Google, talks about getting people excited about the company's cause.

Schmidt believes that young people – students who have recently graduated from college or graduate school – are great examples of people who are ready to be engaged and bring passion into the workplace. He wants them to make sure that they take their mission personally. And he and his associates tap into that by allowing engineers to spend 20% of their time working on their own independent projects. Although it doesn't produce golden eggs from a manufacturing standpoint, they claim their method increases experimentation, encourages risk-taking, and allows them to change directions quickly.

Google is also famous (or infamous, depending on who you are) for their unorthodox company environment. Employees can choose to work in their cubicles or take their computers to large, open-spaced corridors in the building rife with large windows and colorful, plush couches. They also make use of cafés located inside the building for a stimulating social environment where they can choose to work or take a break, never too far from the office.

Company officials have noticed that by allowing their employees these alternative freedoms, the employees have in turn responded with slews of quality and creative work that have helped keep their company on the frontier's edge.

Set meaningful goals

Coaching is redundant if it doesn't have anything to show for it. Coaches are expected to help their employees set realistic goals and help them achieve the same.

The difference between effective leaders and effective managers is that while both are able to guide those underneath them through the assigned tasks and monitor their progress, successful leaders are the ones who are focused on helping develop future leaders. Managers are more administrative types while leaders are more hands-on, encouraging the successes of their team members to grow into further autonomous employees who develop prosperous skill sets and qualities that may be applied to any relevant jobs and yes, higher positions.

Rather than do the work for them however, a leading coach must apply themselves in a delicate balance of involvement that is appropriate to the person's level of capability. Think of teaching a person to ride a bike for the first time – you can support them a number of times, but eventually you have to give them the space to grow and succeed on their own. The focus should be on proper initial guidance.

The most commonly used structure for mutual goal setting in the workplace is found in the acronym S-M-A-R-T:

Specific: Well-defined to inform employees exactly what is expected, when, and how much progress toward goal completion.

Measureable: Provide milestones to track progress and motivate employees toward achievement.

Attainable: Success needs to be achievable with effort

Relevant: You and your employee should focus on the greatest impact to the overall company strategy.

Time-bound: Establish enough time to achieve the goal, but not too much time to undermine performance. Goals without deadlines tend to be overtaken by the day-to-day crises.

In order to help an employee set meaningful goals, they must align with the larger goals of the organization. Employees must develop a sense of positional awareness and see how their job fits in with the larger mission of success. In fact, it is common for people who don't understand the purpose of their roles or practice to become disinterested in what they are doing.

Consider when you were first learning math applications. There were a bunch of numbers that turned into other numbers, then all of a sudden there were these letters too, and you had to shuffle some from one side of a double-dashed line to the other and it all seemed pretty tedious. The most popular question students ask in math class is, "What is the point?" They see no purpose or immediate application for all of this work they are being asked to do. And then an effective teacher comes along and shares the big secret – the purpose of learning math equations is to train people how to problem solve, to notice patterns and rearrange difficult tasks into more manageable ones. All of a sudden a large portion of students regain motivation.

You must be this effective coach for your employees by helping them understand the bigger scheme of the organization to make those adjustments when they get in a bind. If an employee understands this well, they should be able to describe how the purpose of their efforts add to the larger strategy at all times. You are helping them develop that integral scope.

The Harvard Business Review outlines a great deal in effective goal setting. They suggest holding individual meetings with your employees and asking them to come up with goals that directly contribute to the organization's mission. When he or she has offered their initial goals, have a discussion with them to determine if those goals are realistic and challenging enough. You don't want them to bite off more than they can chew, at the same time you want them and they should want to push themselves outside of their comfort zone.

This should be a corroborative effort between you and the employee. It is important to listen to them and their own sense of capability, because while you want the best out of them, they will come to resent you and perform poorly if you push them into goals that are too challenging to accomplish. Likewise if you do not push them enough, they will not grow and your company as a whole may start to lag. Find the balance of these 'stretch goals' for each employee and you will notice an increase in the momentum of the organization as a whole.

The next step after establishing goals is to ask your employee how he or she plans to meet it. This objective should be largely handled by the employee himself to encourage that sense of strength and self-reliance. Remember that you are acting as a guide. Have them break the goals down into individual tasks and set mini in-between objectives to be reached. Concept-check with them to see what they feel the proper landmarks may be. Ask them to consider what risks and challenges they may encounter along the way and how they plan to deal with them. An added consideration is to incorporate what people the employee may be dependent upon to achieve their goals so they train themselves to keep looking at the larger picture. Problem solve with them on how they may best influence those people to see the objectives through to completion.

While you want to encourage your employees in this process to be able to fend for themselves, you must also maintain that balance of assuring them that they are part of a unit, and their goals are your goals as well as the company's goals. Monitor their progress regularly – before they hit their proposed landmarks – and you will help nip any problems in the bud early on. Check in with them on a weekly basis and since each employee performs differently, be sure to ask them what level of monitoring and feedback would be most helpful. Remember that everyone needs continuous feedback and coaching, and the more succinctly you can provide this for them, the tighter your ship will be running.

You want to be building relationships with your employees throughout this process. The more comfortable they are with coming to you when they incur an obstacle, which commonly happens when striving to reach objectives, the better you will be able to help them solve problems immediately or rework a goal that needs tweaking without backtracking too much.

Remember that your employees are people too and have personal lives, so take into consideration what their personal goals are in the context of work. You will effectively get more out of the person, because you are addressing them as a whole instead of just a part of work. Be open and ask them if they have any personal goals that they would like to share with you. They should do this only if they feel comfortable – it is their chance to take a step forward, so if they don't take the initiative when you open the door to them, don't push them into it. You can always provide other opportunities for them later.

Then ask how you and the company may adapt to help them reach these goals. This puts a sense of control in the hands of the employee to own up to their goals. Make sure that their personal goals align in some way to benefit the team, branch, or company as a whole also, otherwise it will become a distraction for everyone.

Sometimes the inevitable happens after all precautions are taken into account and goals still can't be met. It will be your job to find out why and hold the people involved responsible for it. This may include yourself as the coach. Whether the employee was within control of the failure or was not, or you had contributed to the problem in some way, you must find out to rectify the situation or make sure that it can be avoided in the future. If the problem was in the employee's control, have them review the proposed solutions that you two had worked out together during their goal setting and have them try at it again. If it was out of their hands or they were too bold in making that goal, acknowledge it but don't dwell on it. Make sure that you both learn from it for future reference.

If in fact you had made a contribution to the error, be bold enough to put yourself under the scope – were you a bit too neglectful in the monitoring process? Did you not provide enough or specific enough feedback? You must not shirk away from taking account where it's due. If you happen to be at fault and admit it, your employees will respect you more for it by cultivating a well-rounded understanding in the workplace. Have an open discussion about what differences you will make for next time.

The integration of coaches makes for role models in the workspace which builds a better relationship between workers and achieves higher goals.

Chapter 5

The Don’ts for Good Leadership

While assuming a leadership position, many can get carried away by the power and self-importance, which leads to a dwindling sense of respect among their subordinates. There a lot of things to keep in mind to be a good leader, and among them are a few don’ts that will pave the way to being a more inspiring leader. Good leadership inspires people to reach their full potential and realize goals, while bad leadership makes people feel like they are being forced to do something under the action of authority.

Egocentric outlook

This involves a heightened sense of superiority, where a leader is convinced that they are the most important in their corporate sphere, and that their subordinates do not matter. As previously discussed, it is important that you recognize the needs of those who work with you, and not disregard their importance to the organization. Remembering that without having the employees that you lead, there wouldn't be a company to run.

Egocentricism operates on the belief that the needs and opinions of oneself are of a higher priority that anyone else's, which is a quite negative approach. Such leaders see no limit to their knowledge and completely take no notice of the others. It demoralizes the subordinates and causes resentment.

This attitude also clearly exhibits a few other faults pertinent to the role of leadership after a closer look of their implications. For one, assuming one possesses all the knowledge needed for their job puts an immediate cap on their growth. You think you've learned all you need to know for your position? Ok then, you can go home now, you're done.

Successful leaders operate with a sense of humility and awe that they can always learn more about effectiveness in their job, in approaching their employees and eliciting their best work, and about their particular industry (and other related industries). The fact that the nature of businesses are always changing, growing, evolving should speak directly to your own position.

Being a leader means being a team player, putting your employees and the company before yourself as stated before. So essentially without the success of the others around you, there is no success for you. You become the person stuck on the island with no passing ships.

Egocentrism also fosters the idea that one has control over the lives of others, so that others must obey what they ascribe, or they will be dealing out consequences. This attitude effectually harms the one exerting it because by hindering the growth of others, they restrict their own growth. What happens is a stagnancy forms where the constant changing force of the outside world washes away those who are not willing to change along with it.

Invulnerability

Leaders drunk on power tend to believe that they can get away with anything, owing to their high ranking position. In this belief, they commit many fallacies, thinking that no harm will befall them because they are too cunning and smooth to actually get caught. This feeling of being invulnerable and untouchable creates a divide between the subordinates and the leader and they are put into an awkward position.

Invulnerability sides on the polar opposite of building trust in the workplace. The immediate effect is a reduction in progress among those directly involved. This could be for a number of reasons, whether because the workers operating under the power-hungry leaders become discouraged, disgruntled, or such in-office disorder ensues that the branch becomes inefficient. Cases of malignant behavior may permeate among the workers, or simply trying to manage them becomes more difficult because they develop a resistance to their autocratic manager.

Being over-friendly

In good leadership, you want to come across as approachable, and that is great. However, bad leaders are known for becoming too friendly with their subordinates, to the extent where the employees start to not take the leader too seriously anymore. You can be nice as long as you are prepared to make difficult choices when they are necessary, like firing the wrong person for the job, and keeping a rational perspective about it (that person would only drive customers away or keep other employees so entangled in their poor habits that it would drive team harmony down).

Micro-managing becomes a problem when your employees are being difficult and you feel bad about telling them that they've committed a mistake and that they need to rectify it at any cost. This becomes commonplace with the belief or *hope* that the issue will resolve itself over time. Throughout many circumstances that have gone just this way, time and time again they've proven that they need intervention. It's best just to confront the problem from the moment you realize it rather than putting it off.

Bad leaders let their subordinates undermine their authority. They allow stakeholders to take advantage of their time schedule. They give benefit to customers who are loud and abrasive, demanding free compensation when the company policy statement clearly has them covered. Consider this – if a nice leader continually gives the benefit to irresponsible, ineffective employees, the more skillful members of your group who work hard and see this will grow bitter. Is it fair that the more apathetic employees get break after break while everyone else is following the rules? Eventually the better-performing workers will take their own initiative and leave the company. Then you will be stuck with slacker employees that drive your productivity and your reputation as a business professional way down. That is not the kind of leader you want to become.

Be direct and concise with your rules and expectations in the workplace and administer them consistently to prevent this scenario from happening. It may not feel good at first to be 'the enforcer,' but it will over time when you team's productivity shows something for it. Remember that being liked is not the same as being respected. Respect comes with getting results, exerting prowess, and holding yourself and others up to an agreeable standard that boosts morale.

Failing to provide a pleasant work environment

Being a leader entails managing people and keeping them in check, which may earn you the title of a tough cookie to crack. However, productivity increases by a great margin when people actually enjoy the work that they are assigned and have fun in the workplace. It is up to the leader to provide for an easy-going work environment where people can function to the best of their ability. The workspace should be a comfortable space, where people do not find it difficult to communicate among themselves for the better of the company.

Studies in psychology and architecture have come to understand that a person's physical environment has a direct effect on their subconscious and well-being, linked to how well they will perform. Small confining spaces, sharp corners and dull colors are all anti-motivators that mentally drain a person of their energy and wane inspiration over time. How can a person be expected to become creative and innovative on a regular basis at work when they are surrounded by inadequate stimuli?

You may not have the chance to redesign the building structure of your organization, however investing in ergonomic furniture – the kind to effectively accommodate the human body – and arranging internal spaces to be more open and allow for more movement are a few ways you can improve the physical work environment. This means going beyond hanging up the sporadic motivational poster.

A pleasant work environment includes the overall mood of the workplace too, and largely derives its source of that mood from the leader. Look at what drives you and what pleases you. Treat your employees as you would honestly like to be treated yourself. Bring a high-energy attitude into the workplace because you enjoy being there, and if you don't, take the initiative to make it a place that you do.

Failure in proper delegation

To get the most out of a situation, it is prudent that the work is divided suitably amongst the workforce. Leaders sometimes make a lapse in judgment when it comes to delegating duties, and it makes for ineffective leadership. Think about the friends you have when you are looking for advice. In order to get some real answers that would be helpful to you, you would not ask every one of your friends. You would take into consideration past experiences with those people and consider who is more adept with particular issues and who has been helpful before.

For example, are you going to ask your friend who is mostly interested in art about how to design a webpage? Probably not, or you may get something fairly out of tune with what you were aiming for. You will have better results asking the friend involved in graphic or web design. Make sure that a person's skills are complementary to the tasks you are delegating to achieve the most favorable results.

Those who are control freaks by nature will insist on doing most of the work themselves out of hesitation that nobody else would be able to do it properly- leading to unwarranted and extra stress. Leaders must learn how to delegate duties and not try to do everything by themselves at once.

Insufficient feedback

It is vital for the team to be in the know-how about their merits and demerits on a particular project. Waiting for it to be the time for performance evaluations to let someone know of their mistake can prove fatal to the company. If there has been a mistake, then it is important to let your subordinate know right away so that they do not repeat it in the future.

If you do not address problems or mistakes when they are first presented they will inevitably lead into bigger ones. Also, you will have missed the opportunity to address the issue while it is still fresh in the minds of everyone involved so that they can make a more conscious effort at correcting it. If you wait until a performance review to address something that happened months earlier, your employee will most likely take it less seriously or brush it off because the reality of the experience will have faded from their minds.

Does this mean that you must address every single issue when it presents itself, no matter how big or small? No, by then you will have wasted both yours and your employees' time getting caught up in the details. Weigh out the importance and relevance of what should be brought to your employees' attention by considering the bigger task at hand and the interim goals that will get you all there. Cushion the volume of long-term reviews by establishing regulated weekly, bi-weekly, or monthly performance assessments.

Feedback, whether good or bad, is as an important factor as any into the well-functioning of a unit.

Failure in providing rewards

Some leaders fail to acknowledge the time and effort put into achieving a goal by their employees. This in turn leads to a decrease in their self-esteem, questioning their value with the company. All work and no recognition eventually wears down on the psyche whether people are aware of it or not. Job tasks will appear to require more effort, workers become discouraged and lapses in productivity begin to occur. Resentment may set in. Some workers may feel underappreciated and if given long enough, will consider leaving the company for better prospects elsewhere.

If workers are provided with incentives and rewards for their hard work, they will be further motivated to work better. You will want to consider exactly why you are rewarding an employee and make sure that it is aligned with the company's strategy. Would you prefer them to get the job done faster while maintaining the integrity of quality? Would you want them to come in early and spend more time at work? Consider these objectives carefully and then construct a plan to highlight which behaviours are most valuable to your company. Customer care, improved leadership skills and averting apparent crises in high-risk businesses are all qualities to consider.

Then decide how you will want to reward those behaviours. Many businesses miss out on the most cost-effective and morale-boosting incentives – recognition and appreciation. Showing recognition means making a public statement in front of coworkers and colleagues, commending a certain employee on a specific achievement they made. If done right, not only will it provide a boost in confidence for that employee, but it will provide incentive for the others to up their game as well. The other form is showing appreciation, which can be as simple as stopping by the employee's desk to congratulate them for their extra effort.

Orthodox outlook, resistance to change

A dead giveaway of a bad leader is his or her inability to change their ways. They are so set in their old ways, which they find comfortable, that they will stick to practicing those methods even when the future of the company is threatened. Respecting old practices is great, but not at the cost of the business. A fresh approach to things is sometimes the best option there is. Bad leaders restrict themselves while good leaders evolve.

Conclusion

Thank you for choosing this book. I hope it has been a satisfying read for you.

Leadership is a necessary trait for any high-ranking position in any organization. While some possess a natural leadership attitude, in others, it has to be manifested through careful practice and guidance. This book aimed to do just that. Leaders cannot be made overnight, but this book aims at providing you with pointers, tips, and insight into becoming a better leader so you can perform well in the workspace.

Effective leadership is all about providing a vision and motivating your team members to work towards achieving the same goal. There are a wide variety of qualities that make a good leader, as discussed in the book previously. In the book, also outlined, are the things expected from a good leader, strategies for leading in business, pointers on how to coach your subordinates, and what not to do in order to be a good leader.

Acting in a leadership position does not mean that you are set in a role and cannot evolve. Leadership is about doing new things and playing with the possible outcomes till you get satisfactory results. Put the insight offered in this book to good use and improve your leadership skills to get optimum results in the workplace.

I hope you have found the book helpful, and will continue to refer to it in the future to help build yourself a successful leadership profile.

Good luck on your endeavors in the corporate world!

P.S. Continue your education on the next page..

Management

Golden Nugget Methods to Manage Effectively

Teams, Personnel Management, Management Skills & Conflict Resolution

Disclaimer Notice:

Please note the information contained within this document is for educational and entertainment purposes only. Every attempt has been made to provide accurate, up to date and reliable complete information. No warranties of any kind are expressed or implied. Readers acknowledge that the author is not engaging in the rendering of legal, financial, medical or professional advice.

Introduction

Most of the managers today are equipped with skills to manage their teams. Beyond that, as a manager you need something else to manage your teams effectively, resolve conflicts innovatively and adhere to the deadlines every time. This requires special skills that are either obtained by experience or by learning.

This book reveals time-tested strategies that every manager should learn. You will be reading every situation that happens at your work and a better way of dealing with it. It takes a lot of time for your team to accept you as a leader, but if you are able to pull of something extraordinary that the team and your management expects, you are in for a big game.

This book introduces you to a novel concept of game changing strategies that every manager should adopt in a given situation. Time and again, you are expected to deliver and these expectations never come down. Apart from motivating your team and getting the desired results you too need motivation at a different level. You will learn all these and many more from every chapter that is crafted for the manager and leader in you.

To survive, organizations must deliver value. Private and public organizations face the challenge to be faster, cheaper, better, more reliable, more responsive and more convenient. Success today is no indicator of future success, or even survival.

And to do all the above, you need a team that can deliver everything on time every time. This book provides golden nuggets or chunks of process-oriented methods that can be picked up from any page. You can implement these ideas at any point of time in any given situation.

Chapter 1

Effective Team Management Skills

Teams have the potential of exponentially empowering an organization as every member completes the other and in turn creates synergy. Creating and managing effective teams is a challenge worth taking on as the benefits of synergy are a great reward.

In this chapter you will learn and understand tools and thoughts on how to create and manage effective teams in the workplace. Management theory identifies a team as 3 or more members with the opportunity to create hierarchies and interactions amongst them (therefore a large group of people is not a team). There are three distinct types of teams:

- Organic Growth teams – Teams that are supported by an organizational structure.
- Project Specific teams – Teams that are assembled for a specific project.
- Non-organic Growth teams – Teams that are assembled in an organization for a specific process or task or multi-disciplinary teams.

The role of a manager

In every team the manager plays a role in which professional as well as procedural guidance holds an extremely important place. Effectiveness of teams can be described as effectiveness compared to the target set at the forming of the team or as effectiveness compared to resources. What we look for in effective teams is the synergy. Synergy is what separates a good team from just a team and what enables team based organizations to create a viable competitive advantage over time.

In order to create and manage effective teams, a manager must work to enable the advantages of a team to bloom. A manager of a good effective team must use the following characteristics to most benefit the organization:

- Use the differential knowledge of team members – The sum of knowledge in a team is obviously greater than of any individual. Moreover, differential knowledge creates that sought after synergy.
- Enable diversity of opinion and approach – Different team members have accumulated different experience and to solving problems. Use that resource in order to address issues in a variety of ways.
- Acceptance and commitment – Being a part of a process or team creates acceptance and commitment to the team and to its goals. Encourage the team to share and make use of every team member in order to create that commitment.
- Offer team members a stage to show intellectual abilities – Team members will flourish if given the opportunity to express themselves.
- Do not be afraid of disputes – Disputes lead to growth in a team.

Manager and the effective team

A manager of a good effective team must also be wary of the following unwanted characteristics of teams:

- Avoid group pressure – Try to minimize group pressure and dominance of certain members. Group pressure effects free thought and expression subduing great possible ideas.

- Do not let one member take control over a team.

- Politics should be avoided – Do not enable politics between team members. Compromises made using political power harm the team's goals and effectiveness, as they might not be the optimum outcome of a team.

- Keep the original goals of the team at the center – Many teams naturally shift the center of attention to other issues and goals.

- Avoid groupthink – Groupthink is one of the most dangerous characteristics of teams and should be avoided at all costs. Group thinks usually leads to unwanted solutions and can severely harm an organization.

Utilizing the tools mentioned above will help create synergy in a team as a result of mutual fertilization of ideas. This process is as intuitive as it might be analytical.

Managers must recognize that they play a central role in effective team building. However, to be successful, managers require a framework to guide their activities. As a manager you need considerable planning and environmental knowledge to implement certain strategies that are discussed below.

Identify team characteristics before you say "go"

The success of team-building efforts is a function of the number of desirable team characteristics that can be built into a work environment. The actual mix of factors considered relevant is a function of the type of team being formed (e.g., temporary vs. permanent), tasks performed, the team's level in the organization, the length of time it has been in existence, and the ease of substitutability of existing members.

When forming a new temporary team, the manager is normally interested in the technical and interpersonal skills of potential members that are relevant to the group's tasks, the power distribution of selected members, and whether or not selected members adequately represent relevant constituencies. The key to creating an effective new, temporary team is balance in the attributes of team members, and the presence of needed resources to achieve stated goals.

For example, in problem solving and implementation teams, managers must make sure that critical managers with power are selected as members. Therefore, when decisions are made, non-participating managers cannot easily resist. Similarly, managers want to ensure that the required expertise and knowledge exists within the group.

This increases the probability of creative problem solving and outcome acceptance by non-members. In the case of intact groups, where the work unit already exists, management is likely to consider a different set of factors. This happens because intact groups do not allow for easy inter-group transfer and typically engage in tasks that are well established. Consequently, when intact groups are not achieving desired synergies, it is the managers responsibility to identify' those team characteristics likely to have a positive impact on team behavior and change the existing climate so as to remove existing deficiencies.

Creating a team profile from the characteristics identified

There should be a clear link between the presence of positive team characteristics and team effectiveness. Therefore, managers must find a mechanism to measure the degree to which relevant team characteristics currently exist in a given environment. There are basically three traditional approaches to collecting this information: paper-and pencil questionnaires or surveys, direct observation and interviews.

Questionnaire method – the paper and pencil

Paper and pencil questionnaires allow managers to effectively assess the perceptions of group members. Unfortunately, they require significant time to develop and do not allow for real-time clarification by individuals who complete them or follow-up questions by the manager using them.

Direct observation – team and behavior

Direct observation is a second proven technique that can be useful in assessing an existing group or team climate. It requires managers to spend extended periods of time observing, recording, and assessing pre-identified behavioral dimensions and support behaviors.

It is assumed that the observer knows specifically what he or she is looking for and is skilled in observing and recording employee behaviors, In the case of team performance in an intact group, it requires that managers have identified. While this technique can be effective, it does have its disadvantages.

One of the primary disadvantages is that direct observation is labor intensive. To effectively assess an existing team climate can require weeks of observation. At the same time, observation has the potential of altering the behavior of those being watched.

Interviewing techniques

A potential compromise between a paper-and-pencil questionnaire and direct observation is the interview. Interviews allow managers to directly interact with group members, respond to non-verbal cues, and ask follow-up questions should the need arise.

Interviews can also be used to supplement information obtained through questionnaires and direct observation. Interviews are most effective if they are well designed, structured, and ask the same question of each participant.

Chapter 2

Grooming Team Members and Developing Skills

There are lot of ways you can groom your teams and develop their skills for your current projects and future prospects. In order to understand what skills need to be developed you need to first understand what your teams are lacking and then look at those skills to be developed. Below are some carefully chosen strategies that you may adopt for your teams based on your existing situations.

Identify teams that lack in team characteristics

Divide your teams into two one on right side and the other on the left either on a paper or on your desktop. Teams with profiles that fall to the right are likely to be more effective than teams whose profiles fall to the left. When considering team-building interventions, managers should be primarily concerned with poor performing groups whose profile falls on the left side.

Poor performance could be caused by misalignment between employee skills and task requirements, lack of training, lack of practice, or the lack of appropriate tools and equipment. As a manager, it is your responsibility to identify what is lacking in the team and then focus on those aspects till the entire team overcomes it.

Opting for right decisions for teams lacking in certain areas

Given the complexity and uniqueness of most business environments, and the interrelationships between team characteristics, it would be administratively unsound to attempt a broad-based intervention without considering how best to proceed.

In other words: which deficiencies should be addressed first and what would be the appropriate sequence of subsequent interventions? Managers should therefore develop and consider a number of decision criteria that would help them address the issues of setting priorities and sequencing.

However, several examples will help clarify how managers might use relevant criteria to guide their actions. When working on these criteria, managers should already have a detailed understanding of their environments.

First, they need to understand the strengths, weaknesses, interests, and workload of their staff. Next, they should be aware of the history, traditions, and existing culture within the company. Similarly, they need to know what resources are available and how power is distributed within the organization in the event that they need to get more. Above all, they must know their own strengths, weaknesses, and aspirations.

In those instances where this information is not at the managers fingertips, they must take steps to increase their knowledge within the organization.

Team building strategies

Clearly, the actual team-building strategy, or set of strategies, selected by managers will reflect the unique characteristics of each situation. In other words, managers must have an intimate understanding of the unit and the organization. As a result, it is essential for managers to have what the authors call "Ks" in place. "Ks" refer to an intimate working knowledge of the situation.

Without this working knowledge of their environment, it is unlikely that managers will be able to make correct decisions as to which deficiencies to improve first and in what sequence to address remaining team characteristic deficiencies.

There are four data-collection techniques that are capable of providing the necessary "Ks" — real-time observation, review of historical data, interviews, and questionnaires. The first two are day-to-day data collection techniques that help managers understand their micro and macro environments. As such, they are not specific to team building, but rather should reflect the efforts of managers to remain current with their work environments. The remaining two data collection methods are designed to fine-tune managers' decision-making capabilities when engaging in specific team-building efforts.

If a pencil-and-paper questionnaire is initially used to collect team characteristic data, interviews can be used to thoroughly investigate questions or issues arising from the questionnaire. Similarly, summary scores for each team characteristic may fail to provide the necessary detail assessment of what is occurring in the situation. To ensure that this is not the case, managers can review the sub-dimensions or items used to produce the summary scores.

Identify team building strategies that overcome the lacuna

All too often, managers, when attempting to build effective teams, turn to outside professionals to create teams within their units or organization. Once selected, these outside professionals typically take the natural or intact work group off site, and engage in some type of intensive team-building experience.

Carried out in this manner, team-building experiences often take employees away from their jobs for two or three days at a time. The assumption is that intact groups or individuals will transfer appropriate team behaviors back to the job or organizational setting. While such efforts can sensitize group members to the importance of team characteristics, or kick-start an in-house team-building effort, it is your experience that desired behaviors would not often be transferred to the work environment, and if they are, they soon deteriorate.

Instead, these ideas can be espoused by certain strong methodologies as explained in this book that managers can and do play a significant role in the development of teams. Therefore, once managers have determined which team characteristic deficiency should be addressed first, and the sequence of subsequent interventions, they should attempt to articulate available team-building strategies. In constructing such a list, managers can turn to the team building literature, personal experience, in-house experts or managers, or benchmark best practices in other organizations.

Chapter 3

Teams, Individuals and Conflict Resolution

Conflict in the workplace is inevitable. Often, conflict erupts between people due to different values, personalities, opinions, goals, and needs. The workplace seems to foster differences and value differing viewpoints, which are the exact things that cause conflict to occur.

However, conflict is not always a bad thing. It can lead to innovative solutions that people with similar opinions and viewpoints would not likely achieve. The key to channeling conflict into a positive workplace function is to resolve it effectively. When resolved propcrly, conflict can cause personal and professional development that leads to employees who are more productive.

Conflict resolution is necessary in all types of organizations. Frequently, facilitators are assigned the role of helping employees to resolve conflict. Facilitators can be managers, leaders, or designated employees granted the facilitator role in the organization.

The more educated facilitators are on how to resolve conflict in an effective and healthy way, the better the outcome will be. We will discuss four steps designed to equip facilitators with step-by-step instructions on how to effectively resolve conflict in the workplace below.

Meet with the conflicting parties together

This step is one of the most overlooked, yet necessary, steps when employees try to resolve conflict. All parties involved in the conflict should be brought together to discuss the issue at hand. Each party should present its view of the problem without interruptions from the other parties.

It is important for each party to hear everyone's viewpoint and to gain a clear picture of why the parties are conflicting with each other. Ensure that each party states its case clearly and calmly without personally attacking the other parties.

Seeking suggestions

Ask each party for specific suggestions on how to resolve the conflict. Each party should state two to three specific suggestions on how it thinks the conflict could be resolved. For example, "I would like Sally and Eric to provide me with a project status update by Thursday at 10 a.m., so I can provide an accurate project status update to the client on Friday at 8 a.m."

Another example might be, "I would like to own both new policy requests and claims for my clients to reduce client confusion on who to contact for different requests." These examples are very clear and precise, indicating exactly what actions need to occur and by when in order to resolve the conflict.

As the facilitator, help the parties come up with specific suggestions. Try to encourage each party to identify what action is the root cause of the problem. Then, prompt them to come up with specific ways that would resolve the issue. Asking additional questions of the employees may help trigger the parties to uncover the real problem, not just the symptom of the problem, and then to outline a specific resolution.

Discuss the issue and agree to make changes

Next, the parties should discuss the suggestions presented in the previous step and agree to make the necessary changes. This step is where each party engages in a negotiation to come up with a resolution plan. Depending on the complexity of the conflict, it may take some time before all parties come to an agreement on what suggestion should be implemented to resolve the conflict.

As the facilitator, ensure that each party is reasonable and professional. Do not allow the parties to be disrespectful to one another or for the discussion to turn into another argument.

Act quickly to dissolve any discussions that start to escalate into another argument. Encourage each party to give and take to make sure each party feels satisfied with the resolution plan. Also, make sure you remain impartial to either party. Both sides must know that you are there as a neutral party to mediate the conflict.

Follow-up to ensure that the conflict is resolved

The last step is to set a date for the resolution to be implemented and follow-up on its progress. While all parties might feel better after the creation of a resolution plan in step three, the conflict is not resolved until the resolution plan has been implemented.

Conflict resolution is not an easy job. Actually, it is quite a challenge, even for experienced mediators. Facilitators play a key role in helping to maintain a healthy environment for all parties to discuss the problem and reach an agreement to resolve it.

Intervening as appropriate can encourage parties to work toward a resolution before the problem gets out of hand.

In addition, this practice develops your own conflict resolution skills, which is a necessity in today's business world.

Key takes on resolving conflicts

- Conflict is inevitable in the workplace, because companies foster different experiences and viewpoints.
- Conflict is not always a bad thing; healthy conflict can lead to innovative solutions that people with similar opinions and viewpoints would not likely achieve.
- There are four steps that facilitators can follow to resolve conflict in the workplace.

    a. Meet with the conflicting parties together.

    b. Ask each party for specific suggestions on how to resolve the conflict.

    c. Discuss the issue and agree to make changes.

    d. Follow-up to ensure the conflict is resolved.

- Facilitators play a key role in keeping a healthy, balanced environment for all parties to discuss the problem and reach an agreement to resolve it.

Chapter 4

Golden Nugget Methods - Proven Techniques

The golden nugget methods for effective management of teams, developing their skills and shaping them are carefully researched ideas that are meant to be useful to you. Understanding and following these will give you an insight of how to manage your teams on a day to basis and set up a future journey for all of them involved.

Intervention strategies as part of team building

- Goal Setting (Clarify Behavioral Expectations as to Desired Team Behaviors).

- Leadership – Modeling Desired Team Behaviors.

- Structural Changes – e.g., Reporting Relationships, Required Relationships, Required Interactions, Pairing, Task Enrichment.

- Empowering Group as a Whole – for example: Allow for Group Decision Making and Problem Solving.

- Changes to the Performance Management System – Especially in the Area of Reward/Behavior Links.

- Formal Training in Deficient Areas.

- Team Member Coaching by Team Leader or Peers.

- Behavior Modification through Shaping.

- Constructive Feedback.

- Changing Membership (Transfers, Infusion of New Members, etc.).

- Holiday giveaway – as and when required.

Here again, managers are unlikely to have the time, energy, or resources to apply all improvement strategies simultaneously. Nor is it likely that all improvement strategies will be equally effective when applied to any one teams characteristics. Managers should therefore once more articulate and apply a number of decision criteria that would help them decide on the appropriate mix of improvement interventions.

The above-mentioned points provide criteria that managers might find helpful when attempting to compare and select intervention strategies. The criteria are quite similar to those discussed in the earlier chapters, but put greater emphasis on costs and benefits, organizational fit, and alignment with managerial and group member competencies, risk propensity, and preparedness.

Which interventions are selected will reflect the unique characteristics of the situation being considered and the managerial philosophies of key decision makers. As was the case above, it is essential for managers to have their "Ks" in place.

Selecting appropriate intervention strategies

The intervention strategies are based on the following criteria

- Likelihood of Success.
- Cost Benefit or Utility Analysis.
- Time Requirements for Completion.
- Leader Preferences or Competencies.

- Organizational Culture and History.
- Availability of Internal/External Hard Resources to Support Intervention Strategy (Money, Trainers, Facilities, Equipment, etc.).
- Team Member Characteristics and Preparedness.
- Likelihood of Group Member Support.
- Political Pressures and Organizational Realities.
- Impression Management Issues.

Implementing strategies

Implementation is a critical component of any team-building intervention. It is the point at which analysis and planning become reality. Each intervention will have its own unique sequence of steps designed to bring it on line and obtain the desired improvement in the selected team characteristic.

A brief example is provided as an insight into the implementation process:

Preparation

To begin the intervention process to improve open communications, the manager must. First identify what he or she believes are required support behaviors. This can be accomplished through a detailed job analysis, analysis of critical incidents, direct observation, personal introspection, or by seeking input from experts or other successful managers. Output from such activities should provide the manager with the required support behaviors necessary to help improve goal consensus.

Communicate Behaviors

Once identified, it is critical that the manager's behavioral expectations are clearly communicated to group members. This can be accomplished through a formal goal setting meeting, brief informal exchanges with group members, or direct feedback to deficient individuals.

When communicating one's behavioral expectations it is also necessary to indicate why the behaviors are important, the consequences of desired behaviors, the conditions under which they should be exhibited, and how group members will be assessed. The key is to make the employee understand, accept, and be willing to engage in the new behaviors.

Measurement/Feedback

The manager should link the next two steps. He or she observes, records, and rates group members' behavior. When sufficient information has been collected to draw meaningful conclusions, the manager then provides meaningful feedback to group members. During this feedback encounter the manager should indicate his or her willingness to help group members improve their performance through one-on-one coaching.

Coaching Encounter

Any coaching exchange initiated by group members, or the team leader, should be voluntary and reflect the assumption that the coach and employee are joint partners in the process.

The two parties will jointly

(a) Assess current behavior

(b) Try to understand why desired behavior or activities did not occur, and determine if any environmental barriers exist; and

(c) Establish new behavioral expectations for each other. It is at this point that the group member states his or her willingness to change personal behavior.

Monitor and Recycle

No intervention strategy is worth initiating unless managers are willing to monitor its success. Therefore managers working through this process must again observe, record, and evaluate group member behaviors. This information will help managers identify new required behaviors, fine-tune the coaching process, or directly act as the basis for group member feedback.

Chapter 5

Crises and How to Manage a Crisis Efficiently

Crisis management is one of the toughest jobs a manager will have to perform. Throughout your training, you will have gone through the mundane routine so that it is what your brain will be accustomed to. It takes a certain type of test of leadership skill in order to perform well in a crisis.

Hence, it is very crucial that in order to prove yourself, you know exactly how to handle any crisis that may arise in your path to becoming an effective and efficient manager.

Here is a list of characteristics you need to remember that will help you deal with any and all sorts of crises:

Be Critical and Realistic:

As a manager, you are the leader and a leader is never found at the back of the crowd. He is at the front line, leading his team forward. Hence, you should always deal with a crisis head-on. This is possible only if you clear any and all illusions you have about the crisis. Critically analyze all the points of your crisis and plan your strategy according to that. Don't hope for the results to work out. Create a foolproof plan that ensures that you won't have to rely on the elements for your success.

Strategy and Detail:

As a manager, your strategy matters most. You need to see the problem and then look at the bigger picture. You need to look at the wave and see the ripples it will cause. A good and effective manager knows both what is at the top of the mountain and at the base of it. Hence, your vision should be all encompassing. Even if you haven't ever faced a crisis of this sort before, you should know that you are the one who will need to solve it and thus you should take courage in this fact.

This will mean getting down into the fray and learning all there is to learn about it. Get information about your crisis and think about how you can untangle this knot of problems. Remember that your problem will only get solved with minimal damage if you know what cause and effect is. Hence, make a plan of what you are to do and what result that will cause. Thus, your crisis will seem small and you will be able to handle anything easily.

Weigh Your Options:

As a manager, you know by now that there are two sides to everything. And to a crisis, there are multiple sides. Know that there will be many ways to handle a crisis but you need to handle it gracefully so that you handle it quickly, efficiently and without damage to your own goals.

This might mean that you will have to consult with your own team and others as well. Never be afraid to ask for advice. Even if this means that you have to go and talk to other managers like yourself, educate yourself on a crisis and ask for advice. Though at the end you might want to follow your initial plan and do what you wanted to in the beginning, you will have a very clear view of what you are doing and you will do so without the initial worry of 'could I have handled this better?' This is extremely crucial for your own peace of mind since a crisis will stress you out in a great way so you need to eliminate all doubts from your system.

Take Decisions:

Take this as an extension of the last point but you will have to take decisions and take them in good time. There is nothing worse in a crisis than a wrongly timed decision.

To take a decision, you will have to listen to your gut and take the decision that seems the best to you. This only comes after years upon years of experience. A new manager cannot take the best decision because they will always be indecisive. Hence, here is the time when you need to call upon all your years of training and find any instances where you dealt with or saw someone dealing with some crisis of the similar sort.

Decision making, however, is not simply setting things in motion. It also includes you having to sell your decision. The decision not only includes you but also the people who you are working for. Take a decision, detail WHY you took that particular decision and also enlist the results this decision will cause. Try to pick a decision that will cause the least amount of damage possible. Then, go in with full confidence in your choice. Remember that in the end, it all comes down to rational and realistic thinking and hence any decision based on this is the decision that is best.

Collaborate:

Like we mentioned before, never be afraid to ask advice of anyone. If making the best decision means asking help from team-member or another manager, do it. Be very clear of your goals, which are to reach a particular point. And if you think that someone can help you reach your goal in good time and in a better way, ask for help.

Collaboration can mean both working with your team, a particular team-member that you feel can help you in this specific time of need or another manager who might have more experience or experience in a similar way.

Work on the principle that two heads are better than one and if nothing else, you will have another set of eyes to view the problem from. This means that perhaps your decision might be improved or you might find a much easier solution to your problem, both of which will be in your favor.

Collaboration will also help you to beat stress since a second opinion can help you see that your problem might not be as big as you imagined and this will help you reach a conclusion in a better way.

Take Note of Adverse Opinion:

A bad and inefficient manager is one who only surrounds him or herself with those who agree with them. This might make you feel good in the short term but in the long run, you will find yourself in a very lonely position indeed. This means that since you will only find people who agree with everything you say, you will always have to make decisions yourself and you will only have your own opinion reflected back at you.

Avoid this. Keep your critics close because they will show you where you are wrong and this will help you improve greatly. You will never be one hundred percent effective but you always need to strive for that extra ten percent. This means listening to everyone who criticizes you.

Keep in mind that not every critic will be accurate, however. Some people will try to bring you down most deliberately. These are not your friends, either. You should always be aware of your own capabilities. Hence, take every advice and analyze it critically so you neither miss something important nor grow insecure because of the gossip or language of others.

Stay Calm and Positive:

Being critical is the first step and it is a most important one. However, never let yourself grow pessimistic. Whilst in a crisis, you are the leader and your team will be looking up to you. If you get too critical, there is a great chance you will grow increasingly pessimistic. This will cause you to grow depressed which will sap your energy. But not only this, such a habit will affect your team as well.

Your team will be, especially in the case of a crisis, monitoring and copying your every move. If you go into the ordeal head-on, they will be courageous too. If you remain calm, they will feel like everything is under control. However, the slightest sign of trouble and their morale will start to wane and decrease as well. Thus, even if only for your team you need to fake it until you make it. By pretending to stay calm, you will eventually clear your own head and will be able to look at the crisis in a much better way than you had been before.

Hence, even when it feels like the walls are caving in, keep a level head and find your nearest and safest exit and you will make it.

Take Risks:

Timely decisions are wonderful but realistically, taking such decisions means taking a great amount of risks as well. A crisis is a crisis only because you have not dealt with it previously. Thus, be afraid but be rational that your fear is only based on the fact that you have not been here before. This will mean that your brain will reassure itself that since it has faced new experiences before, it can do so time and time again.

Hence, take risks and deliver yourself from this problem. Test waters before you jump in but when the results arrive, make haste in jumping in so that you may reach the results you desire.

As the economic rule goes, greater the risk, greater the profit, you will need to plan out just exactly what it is that you are attempting to do. But when you do take that decision, give it your hundred percent.

Choose The Safest Option:

This might seem easier said than done but in fact, it is one of the best ways of dealing with a crisis. To do this, you will need to clear your mind of any and all sorts of apprehensions. This means taking a break, turning off your cell phone and just writing down whatever options you have. Create a mini feasibility report and see which option causes the least damage whilst giving the best result. Some options might seem to give a hundred percent result but the damage would be great too. Avoid this. Remember that you need to play it safe. Pick a result that might give an 80% of the result but only 5% damage. Ratios come in very handy when making such decisions since you know both what you are gaining and what you are losing.

However, when you do end up making a decision, stick to it and implement each and every aspect of it without doubting yourself. Remember that the time to hesitate has long since passed and therefore what you have is only what you have and you should utilize it to a hundred percent.

Admit Mistakes:

Remember that you are human. You will make mistakes. Don't demonize these. With every crisis that you face, you will learn and get better. Hence, don't try to hide your mistakes; even if you make one, it is a crucial part of learning. Hence, as soon as you realize your fault, correct it and move on to the next step of crisis management.

At the end, remember that no matter what happens, you will never possess all ten of these characteristics right away. There will be a few points that will elude you for a long time until managing a crisis becomes as natural as making a cup of coffee. Also, with every crisis, you will learn more about handling the crises that are to come.

A lot of leaders possess these characteristics naturally and that is what makes them leaders. However, it is in the human nature to memorize and learn. Hence, if you aren't afraid to take risks and are willing to deal with anything head-on, you will be a master of these characteristics and more in record time. Hence, the one characteristic you need to possess in the largest quantity is that of courage.

A good and efficient manager is one who is not afraid to take risks and lead his team through even the choppiest waters to get things done.

Chapter 6

Delegation- How Much Control to Relinquish

Delegation is a skill that is an immensely bitter pill to swallow for a lot of people especially managers. There are a lot of emotional and political barriers that make a manager want to avoid a delegation. A lot of this is based around the fact that even after the job has been completed you will be responsible and accountable for the outcome and that is reason enough to make anyone want to not relinquish control.

However, management experts around the globe agree that once you get the hang of the thing, delegation can be one of the most useful tools which will help you achieve your goals and do so in a quicker and more efficient way.

That being said, it is always confusing for a manager to start delegating until they get the proper hang of the thing. There is, in fact, a whole list of do's and don'ts that apply when you start to delegate tasks to other people. Here is an outline that will help you which tasks you should delegate to other people and which ones you shouldn't even think about delegating:

Which Tasks Can You Delegate?

The first step of delegating is acknowledging the fact that you need to do the hard stuff yourself. Delegation means to relinquish control so that you can focus on more pressing matters by yourself. Hence, the tasks you should delegate should be ones that would be easily handled by even the most inexperienced of employees.

While delegating, remember that your tasks should be simple, quantifiable and easily performed in the time limit that you set. Explain what you want thoroughly even if it means explaining yourself over and over. Remember that delegation is a tool that is for your advantage and not to stress you out further. If you start worrying over delegation as well, that will be the opposite of what delegation is meant to do in the first place.

Here is a list to give you some idea of the tasks you can delegate:

Recurring Decisions and Actions:

There are some tasks that are easy but you still have to do them on a frequent basis. It is always a good idea to hand these easy tasks over to your subordinates. This takes a significant burden off of your shoulders and also trains your subordinates. Hence, this is a win-win situation for everyone.

Priorities That Take Too Much Time:

If you were to go to that list of priorities, you might find that there are some priorities that though important are easy enough for other people to handle. These are the priorities you should hand off as a delegation. Remember that just because it is a priority, doesn't mean it's hard and if it's easy, someone else might be able to do it so you get twice the amount of priorities handled with your combined effort in half the amount of time than it would take if you did it yourself.

Special Tasks:

There is a list of one-time tasks that you will have to perform only once in a while. If these are easy enough that anyone else can handle them, let them handle them for you and save time.

Long-Distance Tasks:

A good manager is always in demand. They will need to be in many places at once but since teleportation has not yet been perfected, that is impossible. Hence, in order to save time to travel, you can employ a delegation that visits far-off places for you and handles some matters so you don't have the additional burden of travel to deal with.

Details:

It is a sad fact that details, do not, in fact, take care of themselves. However, if you can have someone else take care of the details, it is always a good idea to let them. There are a lot of minute details that you will need to take care of while you are managing a project yourself. So, if you have the choice of having a delegation, you can always ask them to keep an eye on the smaller details so that you can focus on the bigger stuff with a clear mind.

Delegate to Train:

You are a manager and a superb one but you are in need of an expert on some subjects at some times. If you notice that one particular team member has a particular penchant or talent for a specific skill, assign related tasks to them. You may start small but you may notice that with time, you will want to increase the difficulty of the tasks. This will mean not only that you will have a valuable asset in your arsenal but also that your team member will be grateful to you for the training.

Above were the tasks that you can easily delegate to anyone. However, there are some tasks that you cannot and should not assign to other people. Here are the limitations to delegation:

Tasks that are Personal:

This doesn't mean sending someone off to pick up your laundry because you shouldn't be doing that anyway. This means tasks that need your specific touch. As a manager, a task is assigned to you because of the way you handle it. Your team is just your tool. Hence, any tasks that require your views, your attention and your style, you shouldn't hand over to your delegation.

Risky Tasks:

Some priority tasks are only so because there is a certain risk involved in performing them; a risk that is only eliminated because of YOUR expertise. A novice will never be able to handle said tasks. Even if they do manage to fulfill the tasks, they might end up messing them up. Hence, it is better to take these tasks yourself just to remain on the safe side.

Have Legal Restrictions:

There are some tasks that only you are ALLOWED to do. This means that you are restricted by law to pass them off to someone else. Hence, this is a big no-no. Never assign the tasks that you are legally bound to do, to someone else no matter how talented they might be.

Tasks that are Specifically Assigned to You:

There might be some tasks that might be assigned to you even if though you might feel that someone else can handle them. These include a lot of tasks your bosses might want you to do efficiently. Remember that if someone has trusted you with a task, it is your responsibility to complete it.

A delegation is a wonderful tool to have at your disposal because it helps you to fulfill tasks at high speed without you stressing out. This also means that you can perform your work efficiently. However, this is never an excuse to slack off on the work that you are meant to do yourself. Practically, whenever you hand off something you are meant to do to someone else, even if the tasks are only slightly varied than what you had in mind, the end result might be a full 180 degrees from what you expected. Hence, no matter what, always handle your tasks yourself and delegate smartly.

Chapter 7

Harassment and Altercations

Harassment is an alarmingly common problem in an office setting. As a manager, it is your job that all your employees feel safe. You will be their first go-to in case they face any problems regarding this issue.

Here are the two most common types of harassment you will have to deal with and tips on how to deal with them:

Sexual Harassment:

One of the most common types of harassment, which you as a manager will have to deal with, is sexual harassment. It's not unheard of, it's not uncommon and yet, a lot of managers, when faced with this issue are at a complete loss as to what to do about it. This is because of a great lack of training. This is why, you should obtain help wherever you can get it from, be it journals or articles, educate yourself. Additionally, if you can't seem to find anything, even the steps mentioned in this article will help you to tackle any types of cases of sexual harassment that you will come across, effectively.

How to deal with sexual harassment:

- Even before any sort of complaint is filed, be sure that you have made your company's policy on sexual harassment clear. Paste notices on the bulletin board, email memos, hold seminars on the thing and make it clear that any complaint that arises will not be tolerated but it will be investigated until either all charges are cleared or proven. Make it crystal clear that your company is strictly intolerant of anything that makes your employees uncomfortable.

- Assign the case to a few trusted staff members in the form of a committee. Head the committee yourself if need be. All staff members should be people who are aware of the company and company's history and should have a clean reputation themselves.

- Make the complainant feel at ease. Even in today's world, it takes a lot of courage to come out with reports of sexual harassment and misconduct because a person is always afraid that it would reflect on their record or there would be a retaliation launched against them.

- Ask the complainant to inform you immediately if they face any sort of retaliation or further harassment either at the hand of the first accused or anyone else. Tell them that they were brave to come to you and that you will make sure that nothing of the sort ever happens again.

- Ask the employee to relay the whole story to you in their own words. Record the interview if need be or take notes but if you plan on taking notes, be thorough as the employee might not want to repeat their ordeal over and over again. Write down anything that feels important such as time, date, place, situation, any witnesses if they'd been around, etc.

- Contact the person accused and tell them that no acts of retaliation will be tolerated. Tell them that a completely fair investigation will be launched against them and they need to be patient until that's finished.

- Assure the accused that both sides of the story are being investigated, theirs as well as their accusers.

- Move on to any witnesses that have been provided by either side and interview them thoroughly as well. Tell them not to let their personal views about either party cloud their judgment. Listen only to facts. Make notes and ask open-ended questions about the situation.

- Interview the accused as you did the accuser. Don't, even for a moment, let them feel like you actually believe that they have been proved as a harasser because this will be viewed as biasedness. Ask if they have any alibis as to where they were when the alleged harassment took place.

- Finally, discuss the results and your findings with other people of your committee. Additionally, consult with any other HR officials and reach a conclusion.

- Decide whether the sexual harassment occurred or not and make appropriate decisions. Remember that sometimes the more serious claims have to be forwarded to the authorities as per the request of the victim, no matter who they might be.

- Sometimes, some issues can be resolved by mediating. However, if the victim feels unsafe and the charges are extremely severe, you might have to terminate the harasser's contract as well.

- Keep a check that this never happens again by follow-up questions and documentation as well.

- Try to restore office environment as soon as the whole case is decided. Do not let your employees dwell over the negativity of the situation. The previous ordeal will have been extremely worrisome and stressful for them too. Make sure that no other employee feels under the weather due to the office air. Welcome anyone to come forward and discuss their apprehensions either in front of everyone or in private if they feel more comfortable that way.

- Take stricter measures once the case is over. Make a case study on sexual harassment and provide your team or department with a presentation. Encourage other managers to do the same. Make posters, powerpoint slides or even get printed pamphlets from various Non Profit Organizations that deal with sexual harassment. Educate your employees on what it means to cross their limits. Additionally, try and educate them on what actually counts as sexual harassment.

- Lastly, ask them for any advice if they feel that the case could have been handled in a better way. Listen to this advice and ponder over it to see if they have a valid point. Also make it clear that just like this time, in case of any further occurrences, justice will be swift and on the spot. Tell them that anyone who feels uncomfortable for whatever reason can come forward at any time in any situation. Also, assure employees that if they feel harassed but would like to remain anonymous, the company will respect their decision and will launch a more secretive investigation for them. Assure your employees that the company's first priority is their safety.

Racial and Religious Discrimination:

This is the second-most common type of discrimination that, you, as a manager will have to worry about in the work place. This is an extremely serious issue and one that has caused many companies to be fined because they have failed to protect their employees against this discrimination.

Racial and religious discrimination can cause a company's environment to turn sour with one group enjoying privileges and power whilst another lives in fear. This gives your employees a huge amount of stress to deal with which means that they will not be able to focus on their work in such a situation.

Here is a step-by-step on how to deal with racial and religious discrimination:

- As you did with sexual harassment, make it clear that your company will never tolerate any instance of racial and/or religious discrimination. Clarify that for the management, one employee is just as precious as the other and any instances of discrimination or harassment based on these topics will be investigated thoroughly and strict action will be taken against the discriminators.

- Train your team to work together regardless of their background. Encourage your team to discuss their problems with each other and come out with anything that troubles them. Emphasize the point that they were chosen not because of their race or religion but because they are talented individuals with a set of characteristics that make them the best at what they do.

- Set up a way in which employees can report on racial and religious discrimination in the office. These charges sometimes prove even more serious than sexual harassment so be sure to assure your employees that they will be kept safe and even their names will be kept anonymous if need be.

- Keep a strict check on people who show up as bullies in complaints again and again.

- If you need to interview an accused employee, do so in the presence of the HR manager.
- Record the interview and take notes. Ask the person's views on race and other religions. Then ask them where they were when the instance of harassment occurred. Ask if they have any alibi or any witnesses.
- Similarly, interview the accuser and make notes on their report as well.
- If you find that the harassment did occur, launch an investigation against the employee and inform them that after the initial warning, this will go on their permanent record.

How to prevent further discrimination:

Once you have dealt with any existing issues comes the step of ensuring that this doesn't happen again and again. For this purpose, you will need to educate your staff and teach them that this sort of discrimination will not be tolerated in the work place.

Tell your employees that they are all humans first and should deal with each other in the same manner. This instance of harassment might also mean that you might want to break and reform your teams with a few members of different ethnic and religious groups in each. Don't put a single diverse employee in every group as this might occur in more bullying. However, introduce at least two employees in each group.

Set tasks that involve ALL team members so they get in the habit of working together, aloof of their differences.

Make presentations and invite independent speakers to educate your employees on why it is wrong for them to discriminate against anyone.

Make posters and put them up around the office. Similarly place notices on the bulletin boards.

Emphasize that anyone caught disrupting office environment will be investigated and dealt with.

Additionally, provide separate contact numbers and emails for anyone who feels that they are being discriminated against. Assure your employees that no matter who they are, their safety is your first concern and so they should come up with anything that is bothering them even if they choose to do so in private.

Lastly, make measures to restore the office's professional environment as quickly as possible. Ask any employee, no matter who they are, to come up to you if they feel like they are uncomfortable with any aspect of the office. Tell them that if they are uncomfortable talking to you; they are free to talk to the HR manager or any other official they feel that can help them.

Ask your employees to discuss their apprehensions freely so that the management has some idea on what their issues are. Encourage them to discuss their problems; no matter how small so that it can be assured that no such events occur again.

Assure all your employees that their privacy will be respected but no discrimination will be tolerated against anyone.

Apart from your employees of a diverse race, your employees belonging to other religions might find that sometimes their religious obligations might clash with their office. Ask these employees to discuss their obligations with the HR manager so that they can allocate a few moments at work for their daily prayers, etc.

As a manager, you should be aware that in any country in the world, racial and religious discrimination is an offense that is often considered a punishable crime. As a leader, it is your utmost responsibility to ensure that all of your employees are feeling safe so that they can give their job a hundred percent.

This might mean that you will have to get up close and personal with any and all members of your team. Discuss their religions, their cultures, anything that makes them unique from you.

This is a great opportunity to learn and by doing so, you will also help other team members understand that just because their fellows are different, it doesn't mean that they are altogether unreachable. Set an example by maintaining a healthy and friendly relationship with any members who are different so that other team-members and office workers might follow your example and do the same.

Chapter 8

How to Boost Employee Productivity

According to various researches, an employee spends more time with their co-workers and in their office than they do with their family at home. This means that because we spend so much time in an office environment, our work is likely to affect our moods and behavior.

Given that the nature of work is stressful, mostly, sometimes, as a manager, you might feel that your employees will start to lag and get tired easily. This will mean a slump in productivity as well. Such habits, though inevitable, are damaging to you and the company. Hence, here is a list of measures you can take to boost your employee's morale, make them more comfortable and so increase their productivity:

Improve The Environment:

Since they spend so much time in the office, your office will be your employee's second home. This means that you need to make their environment as comfortable and friendly as possible. While this does not mean that you treat your employee like a brother or provide beds for them to rest in, it does mean that you should help them get comfortable. Encourage your employees to 'personalize' their environments in subtle ways so even after putting in the longest hours they don't get homesick. Take measures that help your employees stay connected with you. You, as a manager, are also their leader. This means that it is your job to look after your employee so that they come up to you whenever they have a problem. Assure your employee, in subtle, non-verbal ways that you will have their back should they need to discuss a problem that is causing a hindrance in their progress.

Understand Your Employee and Where They Come From:

Motivation is a key factor. Studies show that employees who have to support someone else are both more prone to work harder and more prone to give in to stress. This is natural. However, this can be prevented very easily by a manager's intervention. Some of your employees might even still be students, both working and studying and still supporting their homes.

Talk to your employees, ask about their experiences and then try and relay (in a way that doesn't seem demeaning and dismissive to their problems) your own experiences and views. Even telling your employee simply that you understand their ordeal is sometimes a morale booster. The simplest act of talking helps to unburden your employee so that they get refreshed and a bit of an energy jolt so that they start working with renewed fervor.

Back to the Drawing Board!

Just like you, your employees have been trained to do their jobs. And just like you, they are human. It is a sad fact that though managers get to renew their trainings at seminars, employees don't usually get these benefits. Hence, they are liable to forget a few essential steps in their training. This is where it becomes your job to sit your employees down and give them a refresher course on how they can deal with huge workloads or work that they don't like doing.

Additionally, train your employees on how to deal with and divide stress. Give them points on how to divide work in small groups so that they do it quickly and efficiently without getting bored and losing productivity. You will find an immediate boost in your employee's productivity immediately after such a talk. This is because not only does your employee benefit from the talk but because they feel like their work is being valued. This gives your employees a new sense of responsibility and purpose, which means that they will work harder and smarter than before.

Small Incentives:

Talk to your higher officials about introducing small incentives. A lot of companies are doing this nowadays and have noticed how even a 20$ gift card for a spa or a restaurant is enough of an incentive to get employees to work harder.

This is effective because though an employee is already aware of their salary, they get an added bonus to work for. This helps give them a bit of a fresh breath of air and so they put in more of an effort.

Initiate Discussions:

A tired employee is usually an undervalued one. An employee feels undervalued when they believe that their work is not being taken seriously. Discussing office work with your employees can prevent this. Whether you do it on a personal level by discussing your own tasks or on a more strategic level where you discuss their tasks' strategy with your whole team, this will help your employee feel like they and their opinion are being valued enough to be consulted.

Even if you will make your own decisions, you should try and involve your employees in a discussion in case they give you a new point of view from where to approach your tasks. Then there will be the added benefit of your employee getting their mind off from work in order to engage in something they feel that will benefit the company, this will result in their mind getting a well-needed reprieve from continuous work so when they finally get back to work, their mind will be refreshed and their energy will be somewhat replenished so they will be able to focus on a task better than before.

Be Empathetic:

Your employees are people as well. And as a rule, human beings are very complex. This means that every day, they might be feeling something new or dealing with a new set of problems. This means they though they spend more time working, their minds might not be in their work completely. This is a natural occurrence but one that can be prevented easily. Be sympathetic towards your employees. Ask them questions if they look worried or stressed out.

A female employee might be worried about leaving her children without a babysitter. A young employee might be having trouble managing time with their assignments or exams and work. Although these problems don't directly affect you, they affect the work you will be getting. So it is better to approach employees at the first time of trouble rather than having them redo their work that will only cause frustration and will cause them to lose time. Encourage your employee to come up to you if they have a problem that they feel you might be able to help them with.

Make Their Work Easier:

Don't waste your employees' times by giving them equipment that is slow, broken or outdated. In a professional environment, everything needs to be efficient. If your employee has to wait three minutes for a document to save, they will lose their train of thought.

Make sure that everything from the computer you provide to the photocopier is working at optimum speed. Don't give your employees any excuse to slack off just because you didn't give them the proper equipment. If you feel that your office is lagging behind in the latest technology, order new one. If it's not immediately possible, start off with replacing the most crucial items first but make sure that everything in your office is working at an efficiency rate at which you would want your employees to work: quickly and without delay.

Encourage Questions:

Usually, an employee will believe that they have to solve all their problems themselves. This will mean that even in the occasion where they need more power and more experience, they will try to answer their own queries to the best of their knowledge. This can lead to wastage of time and resources as well. Encouraging your employees to ask questions can easily prevent this. In every meeting, at the beginning of every day, try and encourage your employees to ask a question about their work. Tell them that if for some reason they don't want to ask questions now, they can always do so later.

Drill the point into their heads that asking questions is a good thing and it will help them increase their productivity as well. Tell your employees that their work will be cut in half if they ask the right questions. When an employee does ask a question, welcome them and don't let them feel like you are being burdened because this will discourage them and others from ever approaching you again which will cause productivity to plummet.

Celebrate Your Tasks:

If you manage to secure a difficult client, celebrate. If you manage to complete a task, celebrate. After every job, give your employees a bit of a treat, even if it means giving them half the day off. This is an inexpensive way to show your employees that you appreciate them working and value their hard work in your own way. Not every company can afford to reward employees every time so even just giving a well-done speech will show your employees that though the time might not be ripe to open the champagne, you are still taking in their hard work and would want to reward it somewhat substantially in the future.

Be the Leader:

Again, with the one point that has been emphasized time and time again throughout this book - you are the leader; what you do, others will follow. This means that the strictest person you will have to monitor is yourself. If you are a habitual latecomer, your employees will consider it their right to be tardy. If you slack off at work, your employees will be one step ahead of you. If, however, you are a model employee yourself, your team will feel that they have to work as hard as you do, if not harder than you.

Remember that just like children look up to a teacher, your team will look up to you. This is a good opportunity for any manager to bring his team on track because this means that even the employees who have lost their train and have lagged behind can motivate themselves by looking up to you. Hence, if there is nothing else you can do, start doing your own work the way you would like them to do theirs.

Debunk the Myth of the Favorites:

As a manager, you should never have favorites to begin with. Never make it seem like you prefer one employee to another, even if you do. If you have one favorite, your employees will turn against them and will start slacking off on their own jobs due to feeling underappreciated. This will cause work to slow down considerably. Hence, even if you do have a favorite, stop noticing them more than the other workers. Force yourself, if need be, to interact with other employees. Assign them tasks. Talk to them. Interact with everyone as much as you do with your favorite employee. Make everyone feel equally appreciated but still not superhuman enough to get away with being lazy.

Drill this fact into everyone's mind including your own that your first priority is the office and anyone who works is anyone who will make progress.

It is not hard to encourage your employees to make more progress or to boost their productivity. Remember that every day you will have the opportunity to make a network with each and every one of your teammates. You need to utilize this opportunity to boost your employees' productivity and make them feel more secure in the office environment. A happy employee is the product of a healthy environment and even though you might be a superb manager, you will need your team to build your company. Hence, invest in your tools and hone them for the best results possible.

Chapter 9

How to Bridge the Gap Between Upper Management and Your Team

Sadly, it is a fact that due to some elements, there is a bit of a communication gap between upper management and your team. However, as a manager, it is your job to act as a bridge between these two sides of the lake so communication starts to happen.

An effective manager is a great bridge because he is aware of both the teams' sentiments these being his own team and the proverbial team of the upper management. Knowing these sentiments, however, is not enough. You can either keep transferring feedback or you can build a system into which everyone fits comfortably so the conversation keeps flowing and you never come across a gap ever again.

Here are a few ways to get communication going in order to bridge the gap:

Open-Door Communication Policies:

This means letting everyone talk. Give every employee and person of upper management the opportunity to give their feedback. This is the best and easiest way to get communication going since both sides willingly show their cards and give feedback. If someone is reluctant to communicate in public, gather feedback from both sides via email and communicate it to the other side so that every side knows what they're doing. What they need to do and what they need to stop doing.

Meet!

Holding meetings is crucial. Usually, both sides are completely unaware of who is on the other side. Introduce your team to the management and vice versa. Make it known who is responsible for what and highlight each side's achievements. Then, give everyone the platform to discuss any issue that they might have with the other side and also have them provide at least one solution to the issue they might have.

Recognize Your Team's Body Language:

You will notice when your team is uncomfortable with something. Recognize their body language and have them tell you what's on their mind. Also recognize their style of work. Some might be silent workers whilst others might be leaders. It is your job to get everyone to discuss his or her reservations without someone being left out or bullied. If you feel that one member is being targeted, stop the bullying and assure everyone that his or her issue will be resolved.

Note The Feedback:

Make notes or record the meeting. Take minutes if you have to but make sure that when you meet the next time, no one can point out the same issues about your team. Also, help the other management improve themselves. As a manager, it is your job to create harmony between both the sides. Take each and every member aside and assign him or her tasks that help them get better at what they are required to do. In the next meeting, make sure to highlight the team member's improvement. Make it known as much as the issue was raised so your member's morale is boosted once more and they work harder and more efficiently.

Open Doors:

Open doors that even while you're not around, the gates remain open and members may talk to upper management freely. Communication helps resolve a lot of issues. This is one of the most beneficial things you can do since it will help resolve a lot of issues under the table. One exercise is to give each member of the table a copy of everyone's email address so whenever someone has an issue, they can take it up with the person who is responsible. This will increase conversation and also cause an overall friendly atmosphere to permeate the environment.

Monitor Performance:

Every meeting should be at least a month apart. This will give everyone ample time to make up on what they lack. However, this month should not go by in silence. If you assign someone a task to improve, keep a check on that. Even if you don't, keep yourself updated with what they're doing regarding their particular issue. This will mean that your employees as well as upper management will be both under the impression that their issue is serious and hence they will make an effort to work on it.

When it all comes down to it, your best bet is only communication. Since the gap mostly consists of a communication gap, make sure to keep conversation flowing. Remember yourself and remind everyone that at the end of the day, everyone is a human dealing with their own issues and problems and no one has more power over anyone else, no matter what their status in the office.

This will help upper management accept the employees as people of their own and it will help dissolve any apprehensions the employees might have about interacting as well.

Furthermore, it is always a good idea to have team activities conducted. If you feel that after multiple meetings, you are still at a block, you can always opt for such activities where you divide employees and upper management in groups that have issues with each other. The more they get to know each other, the better they will resolve their issues and the better the communication will start to flow.

As a manager, it will be expected of you to keep feedback from both sides flowing but a smart manager knows that systems are better than individuals; hence it will be in your benefit and everyone else's that you keep conversation flowing in an automatic way so you only have to intervene when absolutely necessary.

Doing so will not only take the burden off your shoulders but it will also help you make a reputation as a smart, effective and remarkable manager. As a manager, the best thing you can do is build a network where everything runs smoothly like a well-oiled machine.

Hence, be smart and start at the base of the problem. Then, build your communication platform up reaching higher management. Bring everyone to the table, give your presentation, start the conversation going and stand back and only intervene here and there when you feel that things are getting off track and you will be good to go.

Chapter 10

Management Tips for a New Manager

If you're a new manager, you are probably very excited about your job. However, with such positions come a lot of responsibilities that lead to a lot of apprehensions. Additionally, there is always the fear of making false starts. If you have any such apprehensions, here is a list of tips that will help you to excel in your field:

Don't Get in Over your Head:

Remember your employee days and remember them well. Try not to make the same mistakes your bosses did to turn you off. You are not the Grand Dictator of the empire and acting as such will only cause you a loss as your employees will not want to perform as well for you as they have the potential to. Remember that you will attract more flies with honey than with vinegar and don't push anyone around solely because you have the power to do so.

Don't Be Afraid to Work:

First point being established, don't be afraid of your new job. Employees might try and take advantage of your meekness so don't be tough but abide your principles. Don't break your own rules to make someone else comfortable.

Ask Your Boss For Advice:

There is no one better to ask for advice than someone who's worn your shoes. Your boss will know exactly how tough your job is and if there's ever a good time to learn from their pool of wisdom, it is now. Ask questions. Ask them of the mistakes they made and try to learn from them so that you don't repeat them. There will be a lot of points they will make that you might not like but at the end, you will find both, points to keep and points to let go. Hence, it is always good to discuss.

Learn About Your Organization:

There will be some things that you will have to do according to your organization. Memorize these before you start to work. Don't be afraid to adapt. Failing to do so can cost you your job or get you labeled as a stubborn and ineffective manager. Remember to keep your principles close and to incorporate them with those that the organization values. Institutions run on the same principles for decades and centuries. Hence why it is very important to learn the culture of where you're performing.

Maintain a Role Model:

Throughout your employee career, there might have been a manager you preferred over all others. Ponder and think hard over what it was that made them so attractive. As an employee start to remember what you wanted, what your manager delivered and what made them so attractive. Try to think from your employee's Point Of View before you take major and especially harsh decisions.

Make Friends:

A good manager is not aloof. Harsh managers are unreachable and though they might get things done, they can't maintain it for long. A good manager is one who is friendly and cares for his team. Don't burden someone like you were burdened yourself. Hold a lot of meetings that let you know your team and get your team to know each other as well. A friendly environment is the best for productivity.

Don't Make Enemies:

A good manager understands that people come from different places and hence different people will have differences. It is your job to make sure that your team leaves these differences outside the door when they step into the office so that no matter what, you are not individuals but in fact one team working for the same goal to get things done.

Ask Your Team:

On your first week, ask your staff what they think is a good manager. You will find some unrealistic expectations but also some practical ones that will help you become a good manager if not a perfect one. Remember that you do not have to be perfect but you will only get ninety percent if you strive for the full hundred. So always keep trying to look for feedback in order to improve yourself.

Compare and Contrast:

Your team might have worked with someone in the past. Ask them to compare yourself with your predecessor and what they did right and what they wish you wouldn't repeat. If you find some habits that are nice, keep them. Let go of unnecessary ones that might give your team a needlessly tough time. Remember that though you are an authority, you need to be compassionate in order to be effective. A team that helps you become your full potential is an asset and it would be foolishness not to utilize the help you're getting.

Talk to Others Who Applied for Your Position:

You might now be in a place where others strived to be. Don't alienate someone and try to be friendly with anyone who strived for your position. Ask questions about what you can do to be a good manager in their opinion. Ask if they would like you to carry a tradition or eliminate a bad habit. You will get your best feedback from your worst critics.

Identify Your Goals:

As a manager, your job is to achieve goals. Identify these and make a list. Prioritize the goals that need attention first and start working on them in order to have place to start off from.

Failing to identify your goals will mean that you will never know where to begin. When you make a goal, you make a priority. Thus, work for your priorities. If you fail to do this, you will likely pull from a stack and the whole empire will come crashing down on top of you.

If you find that you don't yet have an ultimate goal, create short-term goals such as, in one month, three months, six months, one year, five years, ten years, etc. I want to be here. Doing so will help you realize where you want to be in the end. This will also help you work harder and more efficiently like a racer who runs harder when he sees the finish line.

Don't Stress:

This is one of the most common mistakes a manager will make. Don't let the position terrify you enough that you lose track of what you're doing. Remember that you do you remarkably well and someone chose you for a very good reason. Hence, remember to take deep breaths and occasional breaks. Relax for short periods of time and reflect on how to improve yourself, your life and your managerial skills.

Chapter 11

The Qualities of an Effective Manager

As a manager, your work will take up a large portion of your life. This means that you will have to balance your work and personal life at more occasions than one. Since, the purpose of this book is to train and hone you completely; we feel that this topic is as important as any other that is discussed in this book.

What Happens When You Don't Balance Your Work And Personal Life?

It all comes down to planning. As a manager, your job is to plan and handle tasks. If you fail to plan your own life, as is the case with work, your life will turn into utter chaos. You will find yourself both burning out whilst you don't even accomplish anything. This will lead to unhealthy levels of stress, unhappiness and your biggest fear: reduced productivity.

So, if you feel that both your lives have lately been spiraling out of control, or rather, have been bleeding into each other in a way that is concerning for you, be sure to consult this chapter and learn or even re-learn how to keep both your lives separate so you work to your full potential without burning out!

Set Your Priorities:

This is the first and foremost task to achieving balance. Success means different things to different people. Yes, everyone aims for the moon in their own way but while one thing may be a goal to some people, to others, it might be simply, a milestone.

Ask yourself if you could only focus on one thing for the rest of your life, what that would be. This answer, typically, is your first priority. Keep doing this until you have a list. Then, if possible, cut off anything that you find that is unnecessary to both your personal as well as professional life. Learn to de-clutter your life whilst focusing on your priorities.

This will help you to remain focused as well as happy. When you work on something that is your highest priority, you will naturally work with increased levels of interest and enthusiasm. Hence, make a list of priorities and start working on what most closely affects you. Keep in mind that even if you don't like your first priority, it is what needs to be done first and foremost. Training your brain like this will keep you from lagging and you will complete your task easily and quickly.

Back To School!

Remember all those track-team races? Remember how all you wanted to do was to beat the whistle in record time? When you work on restoring balance to your life, you will realize that you will find yourself in situations similar to a track-team race. You will have to meet deadlines, appear in meetings and do everything in a given amount of time. However, all this will not be possible until you are giving your best.

Hence, even when you don't have a clock ticking on your head, it is always a good idea to time yourself and see how quickly you can complete your tasks. This does not meant reaching your office in record time after you've overslept but in fact, timing yourself to see how long it takes for you to complete the first mile on your morning jog. Get a stopwatch and see how quickly it takes for you to make an assignment. See how quickly you can gather all the information you need in order to tackle a certain task.

Hence, start timing yourself and see how many minutes you waste that you could have saved. By doing this, you complete tasks efficiently and with increased levels of focus. Also, the time you save, at the end of the day, can be spent in pleasurable activities to help you relax.

Focus is Key:

So many times, you will find yourself tempted to do everything at once. This is an illusion. Keep in mind the fact that when you give everything your five percent instead of giving one thing your hundred percent, you start losing efficiency. You will never be able to focus on the task at hand because your mind will be jumping to the immediately next task.

Doing this will not only take your focus away from work completely, it will also give you added levels of stress and stress cannot only be cured by simple sleep.

Hence, if you find yourself with your focus deviating, consult the list you prepared in point one and start working on whatever comes first. No matter how pressing other tasks may seem, they can almost always wait. Plus, when you focus on one task, you complete it efficiently instead of letting all your tasks hanging, which will happen if you try and do everything all at once.

Make Room For Fun:

There will be some tasks you enjoy doing so much that you would want to do them all the time. Now, that is not always possible but it is possible to do these tasks at least once a day. In your workday, include at least one task that gives you immense pleasure.

Be creative and you could actually include this in your work as well. For example, if you are a food-enthusiast. Turn a business meeting into a lunch meeting at your favorite restaurant. Similarly, if you have found golf to be your passion, hold golf-meetings to discuss business whilst having the pleasure of enjoying your favorite sport.

These tasks do not have to be over-the-top. If you look forward to listening to music whilst working, invest in a pair of headphones you can whip out whenever you find yourself working alone. Try and indulge in something that takes your mind off the mundane. Not every task and assignment will be as challenging and exciting as you want it to be. Indeed, these will make you feel like you aren't achieving to your full potential when that won't be true. Hence, to keep a positive outlook on life, have some fun while you work.

Respect Your Me-Time:

Pick up any book on success and you will note that this is a point that all the greats have got down pat. If it is time to relax, relax you shall. For a certain amount of time a day, even if it is no more than an hour, set aside work completely. Clear your mind and focus on yourself. This doesn't mean spending an hour in front of the TV, though that may seem therapeutic to some.

For one hour a day, turn your phone to silent and relax. Take a long bath; pamper yourself. Indulge in some exercise or best of all: do yoga. Even by sitting in the lotus position, you will find that your muscles seem looser and your stress will gradually lessen over time. Whatever you do, do it consistently and no matter what, do not let work or anything else interfere in your 'me-time'. If you start working full-time, you will feel like a machine that hasn't been oiled in some time. You will feel strained and as if your brain is burning out. So, in order to avoid this, find some time to relax, even if just for the added productivity.

Step Back And See:

Once in a while, put down your pen and step back and see yourself from an outsider's perspective. Make a list of all the bad habits you have. Poor sleep cycle, bad eating habits and poor exercise patterns might be a few of the major things you will find on your list.

Now, after each item, write the consequence of this habit. This practice is not meant to scare you and make you even more stressed, in fact, it will help you kick these habits. Like when you show a smoker the effects of smoking on the human body, this exercise is meant to show you what your seemingly harmless habits of carelessness are doing to your body.

Once you've made this list, you will find that every time you pick up something unhealthy to eat, you will be thinking twice. You will also find yourself making room for more sleep. Also, you will find that even if you can't devote hours to the gym, your body will try and remain active in other ways even if it means walking home from work instead of taking the bus.

Take A Vacation:

This is an often over looked point when it comes to maintaining a work/life balance. A manager, especially a young one, will believe that they are somewhat invincible and that nothing can hinder their performance. This is simply not true. Even though you might write off your own stress, your body is taking a major toll. This will affect your productivity and will cause you to slow down. As a result, your work will suffer majorly.

Hence, even if it means going away for no more than a weekend, take a vacation, turn off your cellphone, forget your laptop and relax. Try not to 'relax' by doing work-related activities because though you might be relaxing, you will be slacking off even at that. Instead, go swimming; maybe spend a day at the sauna, getting a massage to relax your inevitably sore and overworked muscles; or even just read a book in bed. Whatever you do, remember that just like your me-time, this time is meant to be for relaxing. So even if you would like nothing more than to catch up on sleep, indulge in an activity that you like enough to do it without the regret of wasting your time.

Communicate:

Good communication skills are the key to any manager's success. However, work has a way of taking you away from the people who aren't immediately connected to work. Go through your cell-phone's log and you'll only find a list of employees and business-related calls in the log.

Hence, hit up an old friend, talk to your family or your significant other. If you find that you don't want to talk to anyone like that, join a club. Visit a gym or even the park.

Even the simple act of talking is therapeutic in itself. You don't even have to talk about work. You will find that when you start talking, you will find yourself learning more about yourself than you knew before. Talk about hobbies; think about the things you would like to try someday. Talk to other people about their lives in order to learn about how they keep balance in their lives without burning out.

Set Boundaries and Respect Them:

This is a crucial thing to do. With all the technology today, you will find that you will be bringing work home with you on more than one occasion, in fact, it will be expected of you to avail the opportunity to work more. However, as the idiom goes, all work and no play, similarly, when you find yourself working at three am, learn to set a boundary.

Make a timetable if it helps. Devote times to work and pleasure with some time for relaxation other than sleep. Don't be alarmed if you find yourself allocating more than eight hours of work. There is nothing wrong with wanting to work more. However, when that work begins to seep into your sleep and relaxation, even the time you eat, that is very alarming and unhealthy because it means that you are setting yourself down the path of destruction. Learn to set your boundaries and respect them like you would any other person's.

Find Your Crowd:

If you find that you are still in need of some help, find other managers and discuss how you could help balance your work and life in such a way that nothing suffers. People who have been in the field longer than you will have a lot of insight to offer. Even a new manager might give you something to think about that you might not have thought about yourself. Hence, talk to other people about your problems and not only will they look more realistic to solve, you will also find an easy solution too.

Chapter 12

Work/Life Management-The Precarious Balance between Your Two Lives

As a manager, your work will take up a large portion of your life. This means that you will have to balance your work and personal life at more occasions than one. Since, the purpose of this book is to train and hone you completely; we feel that this topic is as important as any other that is discussed in this book.

What Happens When You Don't Balance Your Work And Personal Life?

It all comes down to planning. As a manager, your job is to plan and handle tasks. If you fail to plan your own life, as is the case with work, your life will turn into utter chaos. You will find yourself both burning out whilst you don't even accomplish anything. This will lead to unhealthy levels of stress, unhappiness and your biggest fear: reduced productivity.

So, if you feel that both your lives have lately been spiraling out of control, or rather, have been bleeding into each other in a way that is concerning for you, be sure to consult this chapter and learn or even re-learn how to keep both your lives separate so you work to your full potential without burning out!

Set Your Priorities:

This is the first and foremost task to achieving balance. Success means different things to different people. Yes, everyone aims for the moon in their own way but while one thing may be a goal to some people, to others, it might be simply, a milestone.

Ask yourself if you could only focus on one thing for the rest of your life, what that would be. This answer, typically, is your first priority. Keep doing this until you have a list. Then, if possible, cut off anything that you find that is unnecessary to both your personal as well as professional life. Learn to de-clutter your life whilst focusing on your priorities.

This will help you to remain focused as well as happy. When you work on something that is your highest priority, you will naturally work with increased levels of interest and enthusiasm. Hence, make a list of priorities and start working on what most closely affects you. Keep in mind that even if you don't like your first priority, it is what needs to be done first and foremost. Training your brain like this will keep you from lagging and you will complete your task easily and quickly.

Back To School!

Remember all those track-team races? Remember how all you wanted to do was to beat the whistle in record time? When you work on restoring balance to your life, you will realize that you will find yourself in situations similar to a track-team race. You will have to meet deadlines, appear in meetings and do everything in a given amount of time. However, all this will not be possible until you are giving your best.

Hence, even when you don't have a clock ticking on your head, it is always a good idea to time yourself and see how quickly you can complete your tasks. This does not meant reaching your office in record time after you've overslept but in fact, timing yourself to see how long it takes for you to complete the first mile on your morning jog. Get a stopwatch and see how quickly it takes for you to make an assignment. See how quickly you can gather all the information you need in order to tackle a certain task.

Hence, start timing yourself and see how many minutes you waste that you could have saved. By doing this, you complete tasks efficiently and with increased levels of focus. Also, the time you save, at the end of the day, can be spent in pleasurable activities to help you relax.

Focus is Key:

So many times, you will find yourself tempted to do everything at once. This is an illusion. Keep in mind the fact that when you give everything your five percent instead of giving one thing your hundred percent, you start losing efficiency. You will never be able to focus on the task at hand because your mind will be jumping to the immediately next task.

Doing this will not only take your focus away from work completely, it will also give you added levels of stress and stress cannot only be cured by simple sleep.

Hence, if you find yourself with your focus deviating, consult the list you prepared in point one and start working on whatever comes first. No matter how pressing other tasks may seem, they can almost always wait. Plus, when you focus on one task, you complete it efficiently instead of letting all your tasks hanging, which will happen if you try and do everything all at once.

Make Room For Fun:

There will be some tasks you enjoy doing so much that you would want to do them all the time. Now, that is not always possible but it is possible to do these tasks at least once a day. In your workday, include at least one task that gives you immense pleasure.

Be creative and you could actually include this in your work as well. For example, if you are a food-enthusiast. Turn a business meeting into a lunch meeting at your favorite restaurant. Similarly, if you have found golf to be your passion, hold golf-meetings to discuss business whilst having the pleasure of enjoying your favorite sport.

These tasks do not have to be over-the-top. If you look forward to listening to music whilst working, invest in a pair of headphones you can whip out whenever you find yourself working alone. Try and indulge in something that takes your mind off the mundane. Not every task and assignment will be as challenging and exciting as you want it to be. Indeed, these will make you feel like you aren't achieving to your full potential when that won't be true. Hence, to keep a positive outlook on life, have some fun while you work.

Respect Your Me-Time:

Pick up any book on success and you will note that this is a point that all the greats have got down pat. If it is time to relax, relax you shall. For a certain amount of time a day, even if it is no more than an hour, set aside work completely. Clear your mind and focus on yourself. This doesn't mean spending an hour in front of the TV, though that may seem therapeutic to some.

For one hour a day, turn your phone to silent and relax. Take a long bath; pamper yourself. Indulge in some exercise or best of all: do yoga. Even by sitting in the lotus position, you will find that your muscles seem looser and your stress will gradually lessen over time. Whatever you do, do it consistently and no matter what, do not let work or anything else interfere in your 'me-time'. If you start working full-time, you will feel like a machine that hasn't been oiled in some time. You will feel strained and as if your brain is burning out. So, in order to avoid this, find some time to relax, even if just for the added productivity.

Step Back and See:

Once in a while, put down your pen and step back and see yourself from an outsider's perspective. Make a list of all the bad habits you have. Poor sleep cycle, bad eating habits and poor exercise patterns might be a few of the major things you will find on your list.

Now, after each item, write the consequence of this habit. This practice is not meant to scare you and make you even more stressed, in fact, it will help you kick these habits. Like when you show a smoker the effects of smoking on the human body, this exercise is meant to show you what your seemingly harmless habits of carelessness are doing to your body.

Once you've made this list, you will find that every time you pick up something unhealthy to eat, you will be thinking twice. You will also find yourself making room for more sleep. Also, you will find that even if you can't devote hours to the gym, your body will try and remain active in other ways even if it means walking home from work instead of taking the bus.

Take A Vacation:

This is an often overlooked point when it comes to maintaining work-life balance. A manager, especially a young one, will believe that they are somewhat invincible and that nothing can hinder their performance. This is simply not true. Even though you might write off your own stress, your body is taking a major toll. This will affect your productivity and will cause you to slow down. As a result, your work will suffer majorly.

Hence, even if it means going away for no more than a weekend, take a vacation, turn off your cellphone, forget your laptop and relax. Try not to 'relax' by doing work-related activities because though you might be relaxing, you will be slacking off even at that. Instead, go swimming; maybe spend a day at the sauna, getting a massage to relax your inevitably sore and overworked muscles; or even just read a book in bed. Whatever you do, remember that just like your me-time, this time is meant to be for relaxing. So even if you would like nothing more than to catch up on sleep, indulge in an activity that you like enough to do it without the regret of wasting your time.

Communicate:

Good communication skills are the key to any manager's success. However, work has a way of taking you away from the people who aren't immediately connected to work. Go through your cell-phone's log and you'll only find a list of employees and business-related calls in the log.

Hence, hit up an old friend, talk to your family or your significant other. If you find that you don't want to talk to anyone like that, join a club. Visit a gym or even the park.

Even the simple act of talking is therapeutic in itself. You don't even have to talk about work. You will find that when you start talking, you will find yourself learning more about yourself than you knew before. Talk about hobbies; think about the things you would like to try someday. Talk to other people about their lives in order to learn about how they keep balance in their lives without burning out.

Set Boundaries and Respect Them:

This is a crucial thing to do. With all the technology today, you will find that you will be bringing work home with you on more than one occasion, in fact, it will be expected of you to avail the opportunity to work more. However, as the idiom goes, all work and no play, similarly, when you find yourself working at three am, learn to set a boundary.

Make a timetable if it helps. Devote times to work and pleasure with some time for relaxation other than sleep. Don't be alarmed if you find yourself allocating more than eight hours of work. There is nothing wrong with wanting to work more. However, when that work begins to seep into your sleep and relaxation, even the time you eat, that is very alarming and unhealthy because it means that you are setting yourself down the path of destruction. Learn to set your boundaries and respect them like you would any other person's.

Find Your Crowd:

If you find that you are still in need of some help, find other managers and discuss how you could help balance your work and life in such a way that nothing suffers. People who have been in the field longer than you will have a lot of insight to offer. Even a new manager might give you something to think about that you might not have thought about yourself. Hence, talk to other people about your problems and not only will they look more realistic to solve, you will also find an easy solution too.

Chapter 13

Common Management Mistakes and How to Deal With Them

Mistakes are a great way to make progress. However, when you go into the professional field you will find that you will not always be allowed to make mistakes. This is when you need help on how to avoid some pitfalls that might reflect on your career. If you are unsure of what to look out for, here is a list of common mistakes that managers make and how to avoid them:

Not Giving Feedback:

It is a bad idea to not give feedback exactly when it is due. Never wait for the 'right' moment. If you see a team-member lacking in anything give them feedback on the spot. This might seem harsh but it will be much better than giving them a full performance review. Remember to be kind and give people ample opportunity to learn. Don't be harsh.

Make Time:

Surely, your work is important. But as a leader it is important that you make time for your team as well. Sometimes it is better to take a few minutes off from your personal project in order to make time for your team. They will be both thankful and motivated that you care for them and their progress. This will also help them work harder so in the end you will benefit from the time you invested.

Keep a Check:

Don't just assign a project and go to sleep. This will cause a great deal of tension at the end of the day when the project is not up to specification. Keep a regular check on your employee so that you may tell them where they went wrong. Some employees might not like this but you will need to do it if you want a project to be completed the way you wanted it to be.

Don't Be Too Chummy:

It is a good idea to be friendly but it is a bad idea to be too chummy with the employees. This is because they will feel like they can get away with slacking and worse. Hence be a boss and remember your place. Remember that at the end of the day your relationship is professional and you will suffer if you don't maintain it.

Maintain Clear Goals:

Define your goals and what you want clearly to your employees. Don't be vague and don't base anything to a maybe. You are the boss and you decide hence make the decisions.

Not motivating:

A good boss knows that money isn't the only motivator. Your team will get motivated even if you just act politely and keep them happy. Remember to be as kind as you wish your bosses had been but remember to pull in the reigns whenever you feel the team going off track.

Don't hurry recruitment:

When you have huge work load you will be tempted to delegate and hire more people. This will end up in loose ends and disaster. Take things slow and don't hurry a process that takes time. Recruit effectively but not too much. Pick smarter, more efficient people.

Not Delegating:

If you don't delegate, you are only setting yourself up for disaster and stress. Remember to divide your workload in an efficient way so that you get everything done while your team gets experience and no one get stressed out.

Not Understanding Your Role:

This is dangerous as you could be both abusing and misusing your power. Keep yourself aloof of employee duties but also remember that you are not a dictator. Remember, your job and do only what you need to do to get things done.

Being Hypocritical:

Sometimes you will see a manager preaching something they cannot practice. This breaks the precious bond of trust between you and your team and it will also meant that you are assigning tasks that you cannot perform so your team will find it easy to ignore you in the future too. Assign realistic tasks so that your team has an easy time completing them without getting burned out or overworked. Remember to keep your team happy.

Never Fail To Get Your People Behind The Project:

Being a manager is much like being a head of house. This means you cannot run a family unit without having everyone on board. Even one instance of favoritism will result in a lot of problems for you and your team.

Hence, never fail to bring everyone from the team on board and have him or her in your full confidence and vice versa. Remember that if you leave someone out, they will never be willing to give you a hundred percent.

Don't assign wrong tasks:

This means do not assign tasks to people who are not qualified to perform them. If you assign a difficult task to a novice, they will either not do it at all or they will botch it up and give you a little-better-than-failed task. Both of these will be disastrous for your overall project. Hence, when assigning serious tasks, play every member to their strengths and assign people tasks they are qualified to do.

Always Anticipate:

As a manager, make it a rule to anticipate the results of whatever task you are assigning. Have a result in your mind before embarking on any new journey. This will help you achieve a goal. Simply put, if you don't have a goal, what are you even working for?

Be Specific:

Don't be afraid to ask your team of what you want. It is of utmost importance that you tell them exactly what you need so that they know what they need to deliver to you. Remember that if you do not tell them what you have in mind, they will be unable to give you what it is that you need from a project. Hence, it is always a good idea to keep your team on track.

Don't Change Your Goals:

Once you have set a goal; be patient and wait for it to be completed. If you keep changing goals, you will leave projects unfinished and your team will always be on edge. In order to put them all on ease, you will have to be patient. If you find that hard to do, keep checking up on them in subtle ways and reminding them to speed up.

Don't Be Aggressive:

If you're too aggressive, you will alienate your team. They will hide everything from you, be it feedback or their problems. Hence, even when you have to give feedback, give it in the most polite way possible. Never shout at your team even when you feel like it. Don't even shout at them when they fail to meet a deadline since humans make errors often. Be soft and reprimand gently if you absolutely have to. Remember to not compromise on your principles but keep your team at ease so they work both with AND for you.

Have A System:

Say, you decide to change one step of the project in the middle of the night. Now you can neither afford to call everyone up at 1 am or forget someone the next morning. Hence, have a system and stick to it. Furthermore, have your team stick to it as well. Be it email, an application or a text message, have a group and keep them updated with your views and thoughts about the project so that no one gets left out and goes about in the old ways. This will cause both a delay and a build-up, which can be bad especially if you are on a deadline.

Don't rely on technology only:

Yes, you heard that correct. One of the biggest mistakes a manager makes is failing to backup their work. Have a rough hard copy of your progress safe. Additionally, keep the documents safe over various different media. Use online websites such as Dropbox and give your members reading access too. Keep your data safe and in more places and more forms than one so you never have to fight a CPU for your CD.

Define Success:

What defines success to you? This is another reminder about having goals and having specific goals. Define success for yourself AND your team. Let them know what you want as a manager and where you want them to be as well. Confide in your team that you want them to be as successful as you yourself thrive to be. Engage with them and let them know that everyone's success depends on teamwork and if one party fails, everyone fails. Work together and take them into your confidence. You will notice that this will have a positive effect on your team and they will work harder and will offer you more productive results as well.

Offer Criticism:

The ending point brings us full circle. Sometimes, managers might feel threatened by their employees. This will lead them to hold back on criticism that will ultimately result in a bit of tension in the short run and a lot of trouble in the long term.

If you want to be an effective manager, believe in your abilities and don't try to sabotage anyone especially your own team members. Doing so will only mean that you are actually dragging your team away from their own goals. Thus, you are sabotaging, quite effectively, your own project. Hence, failure will be inevitable.

Realize that your team is your own tool and if you break your own tool or fail to keep them sharpened and ready, you are the only one who will suffer in the long run.

Avoid making these mistakes by keeping a track on how well you are performing. Always remember to step back and see if you would consider yourself a good manager if you were working for yourself. If not, try and self-assess on how you could improve yourself. If you can't pinpoint your own problems discuss them with your team and your peers. Even approach your boss if you have to. Remember, you will have to work hard to be a good and effective manager so you will need to get all the feedback you can get and you will only get feedback if you give someone an opening to do so.

Conclusion

In response to globalization, rapid changes in external environments, and a desire by organizations to remain competitive, organizations have continued to flatten, decentralize, re-engineer their business processes, downsize, and empower their employees. To facilitate these changes and gain a competitive edge, managers are increasingly turning to team structures. Now you know how to tackle these situations in a much broader manner.

The actual team design used to support organizational goals may include such structures as cross functional teams, functional work teams, project teams, self-managed teams, intact work teams, employee participation teams, problem-solving teams, maintenance or support teams, and management teams. You can now pick up any strategy that is mentioned in this book and customize it as per your needs.

Unfortunately, the typical team-building effort proves ineffective, for three reasons. First, it relies on the services of an external consultant, who is often unfamiliar with the particular characteristics of the business, the organization, and its people. Second, it involves off-site activities in artificial settings that fail to adequately reflect actual work-site conditions and therefore make transfer difficult. Third, it fails to plan for, monitor, and assess the transfer of team-building activities to the work environment.

As per this book, the principal reason for the ineffectual outcomes of many team building activities is the failure to use a critical team-building resource that is readily available in organizations – the manager. Managers play a critical role in maintaining a team climate through their day-to-day activities. For us, team building must be an ongoing activity internal to the organization.

As such, it should be made one of the manager's primary responsibilities, instead of the responsibility of an external team building consultant or third party within the organization.

You are now aware that the following characteristics are required for effective team performance:

- Clear purpose
- Decision making based on consensus

- Shared leadership
- Listening to what others have to say
- Encouraging open communication
- Self-assessment
- Disagreement to certain extent
- Defining leadership style
- Networking
- Active participation
- Developing healthy relationships
- Role clarity
- Open mindedness and willingness to share
- Giving everyone working space
- Learning environment
- Providing all the necessary support as and when required
- Leadership style and management style

The golden nugget methods offer well thought strategies for today's managers to effective manage their teams and enable them to share their future. You will now be able to use any point from this book and just implement it at your work place with ease.

P.S. Continue your education on the next page...

Communication

Golden Nugget Methods to Communicate Effectively

Interpersonal, Influence, Social Skills & Listening

Disclaimer Notice:

Please note the information contained within this document is for educational and entertainment purposes only. Every attempt has been made to provide accurate, up to date and reliable complete information. No warranties of any kind are expressed or implied. Readers acknowledge that the author is not engaging in the rendering of legal, financial, medical or professional advice.

By reading this document, the reader agrees that under no circumstances are we responsible for any losses, direct or indirect, which are incurred as a result of the use of information contained within this document, including, but not limited to, — errors, omissions, or inaccuracies.

Introduction

It has been said many times that communication is one of the most important assets to living because it puts people together. The ability to transcend the barriers of this world and to actually impart your thoughts, knowledge, dreams, and desires to others around you forms the heart of communication. There's something truly magical about getting to know someone and letting him or her get to know you - to express yourself freely to another individual. It's an exhilarating experience and, most of all - it's absolutely necessary for the world we live in.

Yet, there's a fox in the henhouse. While communication is so vital and now, more than ever, communication with others is so simple and easy that children are proficient at it, we've lost something. We are experiencing generations all around us who know nothing other than the world of social networking and cell phones, worlds that don't require that personal touch in communication. Whether you're just a person stuck in their private cocoon, or a person who wants to make a connection outside of their phone or their computer, this book is for you.

What I want to enthuse you with is the sense of wonder and excitement that communicating with others can give you. The ability to meet new friends, strike up conversations and share with others what's really on your mind is what I'm going to share with you inside these pages. By the time you're done with this book, I want you to know exactly what you're going to do to start sharing with the world who you are and why they should get know you.

But, this isn't limited to the shy and the socially isolated. Maybe you're just looking for a boost in your ability to make a connection with others. You might already be sociable, but you really want to stand out and get people's attention. When you speak, you want all eyes falling on you. Well, there's a way you can get that and I'm going to share that with you.

Of course, there are always those moments in life where we're going to have to stand up in front of a bunch of people and whether you know them or not is going to be irrelevant. All that matters is what you're about to say. Well, I'm going to give you tips on spreading influence and getting your words to come out right when you're talking to large groups of people.

Enough of this! We're wasting valuable time! There's a whole world out there waiting for you to go introduce yourself to it. So let's not waste another second.

Chapter 1

The Personable Person

When you think about communication, what is it that you mean? How do some people manage to take a deep breath and just plunge into the waters and start wading toward others with smiles on their faces, while you feel tangled up and unable to interact? Maybe it's one of life's great mysteries that we'll never know. Or maybe it's just a little courage.

If you're not what you'd consider to be a very brave or outgoing person, there's a good chance that you're an introvert. Introverts have had a lot of publicity lately. A few years ago, it was considered a bad thing if you were given the label of introvert. Now, you come across many introverts through the Internet though you find extroverts as well. The truth is, you should be somewhere in the middle.

Introverts are people who enjoy seclusion and the quieter side of life. That doesn't mean you're relegated to that part of the world, but you probably do get scared off by social engagements and mixing with other people. If that's the case, don't worry. Around half the population is just like you and the other half is going to try and talk to you anyway.

The point of all this is to tell you that what you're probably lacking is the desire and the bravery to actually approach someone and strike up a conversation with them. Now, the key to that is twofold. First, you need to get some courage and the second is that you need to get over yourself.

Courage and confidence are very closely tied together when it comes to speaking to other people. Bravery is what's going to get you into a situation, but confidence is what's going to get you to speak. For the sake of bravery, just do it. Going up to a person and talking to them or speaking up in a group is going to give you the chance to really flex your bravery. What you're facing is an anxiety wall when you're too scared to talk to others. By forcing yourself to overcome that anxiety once, you're going to make it easier for yourself to do it again and again. Eventually, it won't be scary anymore. I promise.

As for confidence, you're going to have to fake that one. Unless you're shaking and sweating a waterfall, people aren't going to know how scared you are. By pretending to be confident and ready for what you're about to say, you're going to come across as confident. By seeing that there's nothing to be afraid of, you'll feel that ease and comfort that comes with confidence. You'll think back and say: "It wasn't that bad." And you'll be absolutely right. So, I'm telling you to fake it until you make it when it comes to confidence.

Being a personable person is just about being friendly to others around you and having the courage and confidence to actually talk to them. If you approach any conversation with bravery and confidence, you're going to be able to talk to anyone. The ease and comfort you're looking for will come in time. I promise you that. Now, let's talk about how you do that effectively.

Chapter 2

Interpersonal

When you break down communication to its core, it's going to bring down all other forms of communication to interpersonal. So what is interpersonal? It's the communication between two people and that's it. Eventually, you just break it down so that two people are talking to each other and that's what I'm going to talk about in this chapter. Here you go.

When you're communicating with others, you're going to want to make sure that you're aware what's going on. One on one communication is how most of us establish friendships and relationships that last for years to come. It's a process that most people begin when they're children but over time they can develop anxiety and fears about the process that really starts to hinder them.

What you need to do is remember that you're talking with another person who isn't judging you. Most people are open and receptive to others when they're approached and those people are only going to judge you if you're awkward. So, if you're looking to give your interpersonal communication an extra boost, here are some tips to help you establish yourself as a communicator.

Ask Questions:

I mean this in the least self-centered or judgmental way possible: people love talking about themselves. If you don't ask questions, you're not giving people a chance to really tell you who they are, what they've done, or how they feel about things. Instead of dominating the conversation or letting dead air rise, just ask them some questions and give them a chance to talk.

Eye Contact:

While too much eye contact makes people uncomfortable, a healthy amount really inspires a sense of trust and connection between two people. Actually look them in the eye when you're talking to them and don't be afraid of giving them that extra special commitment during a conversation. People like to feel like they're the focus of the person they're with.

Get Rid of Your Phone:

When you're in a one on one situation with another person and you have your cell phone out or you're checking it, you're sending a clear and cruel message. It says you're not that important to me. By checking your phone or having it on, you're doing more damage than you could ever hope to repair. Stop being so attached to your phone and put it away if you really want to build a relationship with someone.

Engage:

When you're talking with someone, don't just stare at him or her blankly. Nodding your head, asking questions, giving these subtle hints that you're paying attention to what they're saying is a great way to draw someone closer and make them feel like you've really invested in them.

When it comes to interpersonal relationships, it's time to get serious about them. If you want a relationship with someone, then you need to put the time and energy into actually building up that relationship. By simply enacting these very basic and reasonable skills, you're going to find that people think you're a much more engaging, genuine person. After all, that's what you want in the end. So start implementing these changes right now.

Chapter 3

Influence

When we're communicating with people around us, we want to be able to influence them. Persuasion is one of the most important skills in the business world and in our lives in general. The ability to take people who are in no camp or in the opposite camp and bring them over to your way of thinking is something that will help you for years to come. So how are you going to be able to get people to be influenced by you right now? What steps do you need to take to make a difference?

Well, the first thing I would suggest to you is to know where you stand on situations. Before I give you any tips for you daily interactions, I want you to take a day and really examine who you are. If you don't know what it is you believe in or what it is you stand for, then it's going to be hard to ever get someone to stand with you. Remember that all influence and persuasion is about tying whatever it is you're talking about to a value or a human desire in your life. Know what it is you stand for and find a way to make that come out through your communication.

After you've done your soul searching, go ahead and implement the following steps into getting people to be influenced and inspired by who you are and what it is you're trying to do.

Believe in it:

Whatever you're trying to inspire in people, you need to believe in it or find some way to actually and truly commit to it. If the people around you are not seeing your one hundred percent dedication to the cause, then they're not going to follow you into the dark. Having a true heart and a true dedication to what it is you're working on is going to get other people to believe in it as well.

Light the Fires:

Passion is the single most important attribute that you're going to need when it comes to inspiring people and gaining influence. Look at cult leaders if you need any more evidence. By having passion, you spark and ignite it in everyone around you and people are desperately looking for that fire as well. So find what you're passionate about and let it inject the power and the drive inside of every aspect of your life. People will be drawn to it and they will want to be part of what you're doing.

Be a Stand up Soul:

The fastest way to get people to not like you and not want to be influenced by you is to have a moral character that questionable, shady or malign. People want to feel like they're doing the right thing and are on the right side, so make it your goal to be the best you can be. It's time to be an adult and make the right and best decisions that you can. All eyes are on you and you should start acting that way. No more questionable decisions.

Have Value:

If you want to be influential, you need to have value. That's the most important thing when it comes to influence. If you have position, authority, resources or character, people are going to give ear to what you say. If you're at the bottom of the pyramid, it's going to be hard to gain that influence and that respect that you desire. So, get out there and find some value to who you are. With hard work and a little cunning, you can decipher where you stand in the world and why people want to listen to you.

Influence is something that we all want to have. Everyone wants to feel like they have something worth saying and we want people to listen to us. So when you're looking to see what it is you have worth influencing people over, make sure that you use it for the good of humanity and make people want to rally behind you. After all, everyone wants to be in the good guy's corner.

Chapter 4

Social Skills

For many people, social skills are something that died in college, or unfortunately never developed fully in the first place. If you're not sure what social skills are, then you have my condolences. However, we're going to rectify those problems immediately and have you acting like a social expert.

A quick refresher on the subject. Social skills are communication dynamics and abilities that help you in social environments. So, what skills do you have that are going to help you out when you're in large groups of people? For some of us, we immediately switch over into one of two archetypes of the party scene: obnoxious party goer or reclusive gargoyle. You don't want to be either of those. You want to have sufficient presence to make people listen to you and acknowledge you.

So here are several suggestions I have for you to implement right away in getting people to take you seriously at the next party.

Not the Sun:

You are not the beaming light of the party, unless this is a birthday party or a celebration just for you. At the average event and party, you don't want to be the loudest, most talkative person in the room. In fact, you want to strike a nice balance of engaging with people and letting them engage with you. Don't be the center of attention. You need to be an accent to the party.

Not the Shade:

That being said, you don't want to be silently walking around avoiding people. Go up to people that you know and start talking to them. No one wants to cling to the person they know, so be willing to step away. Look at other people alone or standing by themselves and approach them to talk. They'll be more than willing to have a word with a new, friendly face. Just don't be a shadow through all of this.

Engage Everyone:

When you're in a group of people talking, there's usually one person who isn't saying much. If you have one of these quiet vortexes in your group, they're probably one of two things. The first is that they're shy and want to be part of the conversation. So talk to them. Ask them their opinion and get them talking. You'll make a new friend and hear something new. The second option is that the person not talking is probably the smartest person in the group. A smart person talks less than he listens and you're going to want to hear what they have to say.

Chivalry is Not Dead:

Nor is it gender specific. Having good manners and proper etiquette is the best way to make people respect you and feel like you're a person worth listening to. By being willing to be an upstanding person, you're making it easier for people to want to hear what you're saying. So take a chance and be an upstanding person of great moral character. It'll pay off in spades at a social event for you.

Social skills are difficult for a lot of people who have let them get rusty or have abandoned them all together. So take some time to brush up on what it means to have social skills in an actual social situation. It's worth taking the time to brush up so that you're not making a fool of yourself in front of everyone.

Chapter 5

Listening

Remember the old saying where people were born with just one mouth and two ears so that they could listen twice as much as they spoke? Well, there's a lot of truth in that. Listening is one of the most important and vital aspects of communication that can become abandoned and neglected. It's vital that we all know how to listen properly and how to actually glean all the information that we need to from the people we're talking to.

When you're listening to people, it's important that you're actually investing time in listening and not just investing time in building up your argument before you start talking again. Listening shows people that you're actually interested in them and actually care about what they're saying. It's so important. Just think about the people around you who don't listen to you when you speak. It's one of the most infuriating experiences that a person can go through.

So what can you do to make people feel like you actually listen to them and not just glaze over when they start to speak? Here are a few tips to be a better listener.

<u>Hear Them:</u>

When it comes to listening, you actually need to hear what it is they're saying. I know that might sound simple and a little too easy, but think about how much you have going on when you're listening. You have your own internal thoughts, things happening in your environment and a myriad of other distractions that are competing for your attention. So cut through the noise and actually listen to what they're actually saying to you.

<u>No Phones:</u>

I know that I've discussed this before, but it's so important that we need to talk about it again. Phones kill conversations and the moment someone checks or pulls out their phone, they're not paying attention to you. So, when someone is talking to you, keep your phone off or silent. People are going to hate talking to you if you're constantly checking your phone. While so many people insist that they're capable of multi-tasking, it's not true. One conversation or topic is going to take precedence and it's usually what's on the phone. So shut it off.

Digest What They're Saying:

For many people, while the other person is talking, especially when you're in a debate or argument, they take that time to think of what it is they're going to say next, not what they're being told. Rather than using this as down time to come up with what you're going to say next, actually listen and digest what it is you are being told. They have valuable insights and information that you should be more than willing to listen to. Give them a chance and open up your ears.

Listening is very important when it comes to communication. After all, communication doesn't work if we all just go around talking and there's no one to listen. So rather than talking all the time, why don't you give listening a chance and see what it is you can find out. People love to feel like they're being listened to and you're going to find that people are more willing to talk to you when you're actually listening and digesting what it is they are saying to you.

Chapter 6

Public Speaking

There comes a point in everyone's life when they're going to need to stand in front of a room full of people and talk to people who are expecting something great and impressive from them. The only sad thing about that little truth is that there are so many people out there who are absolutely horrified at the possibility of having to stand in front of people and delivering a speech to them.

Public speaking is statistically more terrifying to people than death, so how are you supposed to foster a comfortable skill set when it comes to public speaking that won't make you feel like you're going to meet a fate worse than death when you stand up? Well, I'm going to give you a few ideas that are going to help you to radically change how you approach public speaking and how you're going to succeed at any speech you're going to have to give to a group of people. So let's get started discussing how you're going to make an impression that will last and give those you're presenting to the experience of a lifetime.

Preparation:

I want you to know that this is the most crucial aspect for any presentation and you need to be completely willing to dedicate the appropriate amount of time that is required to do a good job. By knowing your information or your speech inside out, you're going to find that you're far more confident and comfortable in front of people. Know what it is you're going to be speaking about and you're going to find that the prospect of talking to all those people isn't actually as terrifying as you might think it's going to be. Know your stuff and be an expert. That's what your goal should be.

Confidence:

When you have fully prepped and are absolutely ready for the public speaking event, you might be thinking that there's still something dreadfully wrong for you. What every presenter lacks at first is confidence. By having confidence, you're projecting to the audience that what you're about to tell them is worth knowing and that you're a reliable, credible source for this information.

Having that confidence is going to give you the edge so start to project it. Confidence is something that you can totally fake if you have to. If you pretend you're confident for just long enough, you'll find that your real confidence will catch up with you and give you that extra boost.

<u>You're the Expert:</u>

What a lot of people forget when they're giving a speech or they're giving a presentation is the fact that they're the expert. You're the one who has been spending hours and hours compiling information, stories and evidence that everyone in the audience hasn't been doing. So, when you're scared that everyone in the audience is judging you, just put those fears aside. You're the expert in the room and they're listening to you for whatever information it is you can give them. So act like the expert that you are.

<u>Showmanship:</u>

Having a charismatic and approachable personality is vital for you to really draw in the crowds and convince them that what you're saying is important to them. So foster a need inside of them and tell them why they need this information that you're giving them. If you're presenting in front of a large group of people, don't be afraid to let your personality and your confidence show. You can tell a joke, engage them, and make them feel like they're actually getting something useful out of all of this. A great personality goes a long way in convincing people that they need to know what it is you're telling them.

Read the Room:

When it comes to public speaking, you should always observe your audience and know exactly how they're taking the information you're sharing. By reading the faces and the expressions of those that are in the audience, you can really tell whether or not you're being boring, slow and tedious or whether they find you credible. You want to be able to adjust to the audience and how they're enjoying the information that you're sharing with them. Getting the feedback you need in the moment gives you a lot of great chances to adapt to the situation. Make sure that you're reading your audience and that you're giving them the presentation they deserve.

Public speaking is a horrifying event in the lives of so many people, but it doesn't have to be that way. You should really take a moment and take a deep breath before you really start to freak out about public speaking. With the tips that I've given you, you're going to be able to share with those around what it is you need to tell them and give the best possible performance. There's nothing scary about being an expert in what it is you've studied very hard and for a very long time. So when you're standing up there in front of your audience, make sure that you implement the suggestions I've given you and it'll be a piece of cake for you and you'll blow those fears out of the water.

Chapter 7

Learning to Trust Others (and Yourself)

There is usually no single reason that a person is unable to communicate successfully. One of the major reasons why you might be unable to communicate successfully or why you may not be able to articulate yourself is that you are unable to trust other people. You feel as though they will not understand what you have to say, or will perhaps mock it for being somehow uninteresting or unintellectual.

This is obviously not a reflection of your own character. It is usually an impression you have of yourself that you project onto other people, believing that these other people that you are attempting to communicate with will believe that you are as inadequate as you believe yourself to be.

A mistrust of others can also result from feeling as though they are adequate recipients of your communications. You may feel that they are in some way untrustworthy, that they are bad people or that they do not have your back. This lack of trust is natural, it is the result of bad experiences that you may have gone through in your life, or perhaps it just naturally how you are. Whatever the cause of this mistrust of others, it stops you from communicating effectively, and so must be tackled if you ever hope to start communicating in a way that will get what you are trying to say across.

It is not just others that you might not be able to trust. Very often, people that have difficulty communicating often have trust issues with themselves. Many people would be surprised by this concept. How can one mistrust oneself? After all, there is nothing more concrete than one's own personality. However, since you are reading this book, you are probably aware that this is not the case. Often there is nothing more uncertain than one's own self.

Not trusting yourself means not trusting that you will say the right things. Often when people that don't trust others to appreciate what they have to say, these same people don't believe that they have anything important to say themselves. This lack of trust results in them not saying much as all.

Chances are that you are one of these people. As you can plainly see, trust is a huge part of communication. Trusting others; trusting oneself. These things actually affect one's ability to communicate. Hence, logic dictates that if you want to communicate in a manner that is more efficient, you will have to learn trust others as well as yourself. How, though, can one learn to trust others? How can one learn to trust oneself? Such things are obviously not going to come easily, but if you are willing to work at it there are ways that by which you can overcome your issues with trust.

The first thing that you would need to do in order to get past your issues with trust is to understand the reason behind them. Any learned man would tell you that in order to solve a problem, one must delve into and find its root cause. For it is in the understanding of a problem that one can begin to fix it a step at a time.

The first major cause of a lack of trust in others for you can be that you just are this way naturally. This low propensity of trust itself may have been caused by a variety of factors. A major factor that results in a low propensity to trust is the lack of positive role models while growing up. Perhaps your parents frequently let you down; perhaps you had a relative, a teacher, a friend or a sibling that you felt you could depend on that betrayed your trust by not being there when you needed them to be.

Similarly, childhood trauma is also often a cause of a lack of a desire to trust in others. It has been found in researches conducted on people who suffered abuse over the course of their lives, particularly while they were still children, are often less able to trust people than those who have not suffered any kind of abuse in their lives. Long-term emotional abuse results in you not being willing to hand your trust to other people because, growing up, all the people that you knew and who knew you would only betray your trust.

This links up with the second major cause of a lack of trust: past trauma. Past trauma, if it was serious enough, can result in some major deficiencies in one's personality. One tends to have low self-esteem, something that often results in a lack of trust in oneself. This low self-esteem usually stems from the fact that one blames oneself for the trauma one suffered. This is most often seen in rape victims, who incidentally are not very good at communicating after their trauma either.

Past trauma also often results in one treating oneself as a victim. This leads to a major shift in personality as well, which obviously affects one's communication skills. When you look at yourself as a victim, you tend to look at others as potential offenders. Your entire life becomes based around this paranoia, and mired in such paranoia you are completely unable to trust others. You are unwilling to communicate with people because you feel as though they will not understand your pain, and thus the communication will be worthless to undertake. This is a toxic personality trait. Despite your suffering, you will have to overcome this self-victimization if you can ever hope to begin communicating effectively.

The third major reason that you might not be able to trust others or yourself is, quite simply, your expectations are too high. You want people to act a certain way, and when they don't act that way, the person in question feels betrayed. This is most often seen in relationships. Unrealistic expectations, or expectations that are not overtly spoken or are unclear, will probably never be met.

People often have such unrealistic expectations about themselves as well. A man may expect himself to be a certain kind of masculine, a woman may expect herself to be dainty and soft spoken, and when these people fail to meet their expectations of themselves they begin to stop trusting themselves. They fail to communicate successfully because they feel like they are worth less than they should be. They project their expectations of themselves onto others, and since they don't meet these expectations, they will feel as though they are disappointments to other people. This will result in them not communicating successfully.

This often results in the creation of a vicious cycle. Lack of communication leads to a betrayal of trust, and the cycle goes on. The best way to cure your lack of trust is to break this cycle. You must learn to trust others. You must be wondering how you can even begin to do this, but the process is actually fairly simple. You just need to be willing to work hard at it!

Here are several ways that you can start trusting people once again:

- Let the fear in. You are obviously afraid of letting someone in. You must accept this fear, own it. You must make it a part of you. Once you acknowledge that you are afraid, your fear will be a tangible thing, something that can be objectively analyzed and tackled. Once it has been objectively analyzed you can do something wonderful with it: you can accept it. Acceptance of this fear is a thing so beautiful because it allows you to be comfortable with yourself, which if nothing else, would allow you to become comfortable in your own skin and begin trusting yourself for a change.

- Start cleaning up your act. People often don't communicate because they feel as though others won't think much of them. This is usually due to the fact that they don't think much of themselves. Since you are probably one of these people, how can you start to think better about yourself? Well, you need to get it together. Start being punctual, clean up your place of residence, stop sleeping so much and get some exercise. Other things you can do are to avoid alcohol and food that is not good for you. These things will boost your self-esteem, which in turn will help you feel more confident with yourself. You're probably seeing a pattern emerge here between trusting oneself and beginning to communicate better. Gaining self-confidence is the best way to begin trusting oneself, and cleaning up your act is the best way to gain confidence.

- Socialize. Everybody has friends, even if they just have one or two. If you want to communicate better, it is absolutely essential that you meet with these friends as much as possible. Whether they are just casual get togethers at a local cafe or full fledged nights out partying, the more you socialize the more you're going to start trusting others. Don't have any friends at all? Join some kind of club! It doesn't have to be anything fancy, just a book club will do. Alternatively, you can start taking dancing lessons!

- Accept blame as well as apologies. You are not perfect, and neither is anyone else. There will be moments where you make mistakes. Accept the blame for these mistakes, and try to improve yourself so that others can trust you. Others trusting you will boost your self-confidence and can really help you communicate better! On the other hand, it is also extremely important to forgive those that have hurt you. You are invariably going to be hurt over the course of your life, and the people that hurt you are going to want to apologize. The first step to trusting others is forgiving them for their flaws.

- Learn to love yourself. Everyone is self-deprecating to some degree, so you should feel guilty for criticizing yourself. However, drowning your inner consciousness in a sea of negativity is not exactly healthy. It will sap your self-confidence and leave you feeling worthless. Balance out the negativity with the occasional smidgen of positivity. Find praiseworthy characteristics to your personality or your physical appearance and think to yourself, "This is a good thing about me, I appreciate this aspect of myself." This will help you become more confident which will in turn help you open up and communicate better!

- Don't take things so seriously. Work is work. It is important, but it is only one aspect of your life. So are your romantic relationships. Certain aspects of your life often leave you feeling enraged. You need to overcome these strong emotions if you can ever hope to achieve any significant boost in your confidence whatsoever. Learn to control your anger, your sadness and your impatience. Learn not to take things so seriously and you will definitely start feeling like your communication levels are improving when they aren't impaired by powerful emotions!

- Take it a step at a time. This is possibly the single most important thing that you can do in order to start communicating in a more effective way. Just saying hello to somebody is a significant step. Being able to trust someone with the keys to your home is a major step. However, you should always take this journey a step at a time. Focus on opening up about yourself piece by piece. Tell someone your favorite color, a dream you had last night, what you did or didn't like about your parents. Before you know it, you will be communicating with the best of them.

Chapter 8

Learning to be Honest

Honesty is perhaps just as important a factor in one's communication skills as trust. These two are, in many ways, intertwined, not least of all because one almost always leads into the other.

Miscommunication is a blanket term that can be used to describe any kind of communication that is in any way faulty or dysfunctional. Any type of communication that causes problems is essentially miscommunication. One of the biggest forms and causes of miscommunication is dishonesty. Hence, honesty and a lack thereof must be considered an essential form of communication as a whole.

In order to understand what honesty is, and how one can attempt to be honest in general, one must also strive to understand dishonesty as well. You must understand that there are several forms of dishonesty, and several variations of these forms. Dishonesty is the absence of honesty in communication, and this term can be applied to many, many things.

Lying is perhaps the most pervasive form of dishonesty in human society. You can lie for a variety of reasons. Perhaps there is financial gain in the lie, perhaps there is upward social mobility. You might lie in order to avoid a punishment for something that you have done, in which case you would claim that it was not you who did it. We lie to others for a lot of reasons, but it also very important to realize that we also lie to ourselves.

How exactly do we lie to ourselves? We tell ourselves that something we are doing is not wrong, that it is excusable. We also lie to ourselves to justify our mistreatment of other people. We can lie to ourselves and tell ourselves that we are actually good at communicating, that it is everyone else who is at fault.

Therein lies the fundamental importance of honesty within the realm of communication. A lack of honesty is perhaps the single greatest impediment to the improvement of your communication skills. Hence, it is pretty clear that in order to communicate better, you're going to have to learn how to be honest.

Being Honest With Others

Communicating successfully means being honest, but it also means knowing *how* to be honest. Remember, a lot of the time people don't want honesty. They want you to deceive them in order to make them feel better about themselves. It is absolutely essential that you humor them in this regard. After all, if you were not looking particularly good on a certain day, would you want someone to be blunt and honest and tell you look ugly? Perhaps you were unable to shower because you woke up late. Perhaps you did not have time to look in the mirror in the morning. Whatever the case may be, you are not going to feel good about yourself after someone heartlessly tells you that you don't look good, no matter how honest they were being.

Yet, honesty is an important part of communication. You would not lie about owing someone money or about whether you are capable of a certain task or not. Where then is the line drawn? Human suffering, of course. You do not lie when the lie will cause someone else pain, and you do lie when someone's happiness or self-esteem is at stake. However, this line is a difficult one to see sometimes. In order to help you maintain a level of honesty that is conducive to healthy and efficient communication, here are a few tips:

- Start small: chances are you are not a very honest person. This is not a reflection of your character; perhaps you've been brought up in a way that you had to include small falsehoods into your everyday speech. If this is the case, it's best not to bite off more than you can chew, since you won't know just how honest to be and what type of honesty would best suit a certain situation. Start becoming honest by, for example, telling your friends that you can't make it to a get together because you don't feel like it rather than lying and saying that you are feeling under the weather.

- Don't put honesty off for later: if you have become used to lying, even small white lies, these falsehoods will have become easy by now. They will have become the easy way of getting out of difficult conversations. If you are looking to start communicating more effectively, honesty should be high on your list of priorities, and thus these difficult conversations must be had. However, since they are not the easy way out you might feel like procrastinating and putting the honesty off for later. This is unacceptable. Face your dishonesty like a man and get the truth off your chest. Do this often enough and you will soon find your communication skills will have improved drastically!

- When white lies are okay: there are obviously certain situations where white lies are okay. A white lie is essentially a lie that does not majorly deceive somebody and thus will not result in anybody getting hurt. However, it is important to know just when and where white lies are for the greater good, as telling them too often and for personal gain is just another form of miscommunication and is detrimental to your progress. Whenever honesty is both unnecessary and would probably end up hurting the other person, it's probably better to keep that information to yourself and tell a white lie instead. For example, if your girlfriend asks you if you think she is fat. She is probably feeling self conscious because of impossible beauty standards imposed on her by the media, so telling a lie to make her feel better is actually the right thing to do.

- Don't be too blunt: there is a difference between honesty and bluntness. For example, if your friend wants an honest opinion on the spray tan he is using, saying "It looks terrible!" is very blunt and would probably hurt his feelings. Try to be subtle in your honesty in this regard. Instead of saying outright that the spray tan looks terrible, subtly suggest that it doesn't suit them for some reason or the other. This way, you are being honest, as you have been asked to be, but at the same time you are safeguarding that person's feelings and ensuring that you don't hurt them. Remember, blunt honesty may not be as bad as dishonesty, but it is dysfunctional communication at best and so should be worked on in order to start communicating in more effective manner.

- Remember the importance of apologizing: there is no shame in having been dishonest, even if your dishonesty stretched over a long period of time, as long as you are now taking steps to ensure that you are no longer dishonest. If you have been dishonest for a long time, your natural escape mechanism after having made a mistake will probably be lying in order to make the person you have wronged either believe that the mistake was not your fault or that it was somehow justified. This is obviously the wrong thing to do. The right thing to do would be to tell the truth and apologize for your mistake. You may think that this would get you into trouble, but in general people appreciate that you respected them enough to be honest and apologize for what you have done. Additionally, you will not have to go through the guilt that stems from having deceived someone!

- Keep the option of private honesty in mind: often, people are dishonest simply because they are too embarrassed to admit their problem in a public forum. There are also certain situations where being honest in a public forum is simply not a good thing to do, situations where the honesty that you must display is too embarrassing for the person it pertains to. For example, if you have a friend whose significant other is cheating on them, being honest with them and telling them about it in public would probably be an extremely embarrassing experience for them. Similarly, saying loudly and in public that your friend has something between their teeth would also be embarrassing, despite the fact that you were just being honest. Being honest in private is the preferred form of honesty in these situations. Remember, honesty is a good thing when it is helping the other person, so privately being honest with people about things that might hurt them is an important part of being tactful.

- Honesty requires explanation: there are obviously certain situations where honesty is absolutely necessary. An example of such a situation is the aforementioned situation where you have a friend whose significant other is being unfaithful to them. In such situations it is usually important to be both discreet and reveal your honesty to the person in private as well as explain the reason for your honesty. Make it absolutely clear that you are not being honest to hurt them; you are being honest because you want to be a good person and tell them what they need to know. Honesty must never be used as a weapon and you shouldn't use it in this manner.

- Honesty with an emphasis on the positive is a good thing. People often ask for advice, and in the vast majority of situations would appreciate it if you were honest while providing the advice. This is going to put you in a lot of situations where you have to be honest with the other person and make a negative comment about their appearance or a project that they might be working on. Remember that, although they were asking for honesty, they weren't asking for rudeness or to be put down. When you have to say something negative for the purpose of being honest, try to pad this negativity with a lot of positivity. Tell the person who has asked for your honest opinion that your opinion is a negative one, but it is not their fault or it is a natural part of being at the skill level they are at. In all things, making people feel good about themselves is an essential part of communicating successfully. Since honesty is such an important part of communicating in an effective manner, this applies to this situation as well.

- Don't always assume you're right. Whenever you give somebody an honest opinion, remember that that's exactly what it is, an opinion. Just because you're being honest about the way you feel about something does not mean that what you are saying automatically becomes fact. On the contrary, it is just another honest opinion. People will either choose to take it seriously or they won't and you will have to respect their decision either way. Many people make the serious blunder of getting offended whenever an opinion that they provide is not acted on or taken seriously. Nobody owes it to you to take your opinion seriously. You are being honest for yourself in such situations, and other people are free to accept your honesty and appreciate you for it but not act on it.

- Always think about what you are about to say. Do unto others what you expect for yourself, or so the saying goes. This is perhaps the most basic rule in the entire world of communication. Think before you talk. Whenever you are talking to somebody, mull over the words that you are going to say before actually saying them. Ask yourself "Are these words harsh or blunt? Are you being dishonest without realizing it?" All in all, just try your best to speak to people the way you would like to be spoken to yourself. As long as you follow this one simple rule, you will find that soon your communication skills will have improved and you will have automatically started to become a lot more honest when it is needed and it counts!

Chapter 9

How to Communicate Better in a Relationship

Communication is an important part of each and every aspect of our lives. From our work life to our social lives, the way we communicate dictates everything from our social mobility to our status at work and any potential promotions we might receive. However, in no aspect of our lives is communication more important than in our relationships.

Relationships are bonds between you and other people. Such two person bonds simply cannot exist if a large amount of communication does not take place between them. After all, it is this communication that helps us form these bonds in the first place and find common ground that serves as the basis of the relationship.

Relationships include those that we are born with, such as our relationships with our parents, as well as those that we choose to become part of, such as romantic relationships and friendships. In all of these relationships, proper communication is absolutely necessary.

Often, these relationships fail specifically due to the fact that communication between the two vested parties isn't working. Forms of miscommunication such as lying, angry outbursts and other similar methods of communication, which really don't get any kind of positive message across harm our relationships. They can often damage a relationship in ways that are entirely irreparable.

Hence, it is probably clear to you by now that in order to maintain the relationships you are a part of, you are going to have to start communicating more effectively. You may be wondering how you can start communicating better or how you can improve your relationship by creating a dialogue between you and the person you are in a relationship with. There are several ways that you can do this.

Spend Time Together

Spend time together. Don't just sit in front of the TV and watch repeats of boring shows. Don't just sit next to each other, superficially together, but actually buried deep into the digital world of your smartphone. Take some time out to be together and actually talk. Listen to what the other person has to say, give your input about whether you think what they are saying is right or wrong. Listen, respond, argue, talk and communicate!

This helps in a lot of ways. First of all, you learn how to effectively get what you are saying across to the person you love because they react to what you say and how you say it. You can modify the way you say certain things and avoid saying other things altogether in order to start communicating in a way that is more effective and efficient. You also learn how other people communicate. If you have difficulty communicating in an efficient manner, you need to realize that the best way to start communicating effectively is to listen to how other people communicate. You can apply the communication techniques that other people use in your own communications. Spending time with the people you are in relationships with is a great way to improve your communication skills overall and helps keep the relationships healthy to boot.

Leave Your Ego at the Door

A major cause of miscommunication between two partners, friends or relatives is that their individual egos cause too much strife and result in the wrong things being said. People tend to take things personally. Certain comments seem to make partners in a relationship feel as though their sense of self-worth is somehow being questioned or lowered.

You need to realize that everything is not about you. Certain comments made by your significant other or friend might leave you feeling slighted, but you need to realize that it is highly unlikely that they said what they said in order to hurt you.

This is one of the most common forms of miscommunication between two people who are in some form of a relationship. The presence of an overly large ego usually results in one of the parties taking a certain comment the wrong way. The fact of the matter is that a relationship is a two-way road. If you feel like something your partner or friend has said has somehow offended you, you need to talk to them about it.

The gist is, get over yourself. If you are hurt by something, communicate about it. Don't get trapped in your ego and think that the other person somehow owes it to you to figure out what they have done or said in the first place. If you want to start communicating better, you need to start communicating yourself, your ego be damned.

Avoid Resentment Stemming From Lack of Communication

You may feel that in certain situations your partner or friend says or does something that offends you in some way. Perhaps they said something about the way you look, perhaps they commented on a project that you were undertaking and subtly criticized it. Maybe they did so intentionally, maybe they didn't. Since you have difficulty communicating in an effective manner, something tells me that you won't be communicating your feelings to them any time soon.

There are probably quite a few reasons for this. First and foremost, you may feel as though your opinions are not noteworthy. You may assume that whatever they said you deserved, probably as a result of your low self-esteem. You might also believe that you cannot communicate the way you are feeling simply because your significant other will not understand what you are trying to say. Perhaps you feel as though they will think you weak for getting upset over something so ostensibly, small. Being brought up with a certain sense of masculinity can often do that to a man.

However, it is very important that you realize that your lack of communication in this regard is detrimental to your relationship. Your significant other will never know that a particular comment hurt you and would repeatedly make the same mistake again. You will never be able to ascertain whether the things they had said were intentionally hurtful or if they had simply made a mistake. Eventually, hurt will turn to resentment and the relationship will subsequently deteriorate past the point of reparation. All of this can be prevented if you just take that brave first step and let your significant other know that what they did or said hurt you.

This Is Not a Competition

Over the course of any relationship, you and your significant other, or you friend, are definitely going to argue. This is not a possibility. It is an absolute certainty. Two people coming together in a relationship will almost certainly have a difference in opinion, which will almost certainly result in a clash of personalities.

This is nothing to worry about. It is simply a natural part of every human relationship. After all, pretty much every human being is fundamentally different. Even if you find somebody who shares a lot of your opinions and tastes, there are going to be moments, several of them in fact, in which you disagree, and these moments will most often lead to arguments. In this manner, arguments are actually quite healthy. They help you and your significant other get past these fundamental differences and ease the tension that is invariably present.

Hence, argument is a fundamental part of communication. However, how you approach argument is extremely important. In too many situations, couples approach arguments in the worst way possible. They treat them like competitions. Your relationship is a bond that has been created for the purpose of mutual growth. Your arguments are not competitions that you can win. Listen to what your significant other has to say and get them to listen to what you have to say. This is how you are going to start improving your communication skills and your relationship as well.

Respect opinions

Chances are, you are a person with strong opinions. You believe that Coke tastes better than Pepsi, basketball is the greatest sport in the world or that Radiohead is the greatest band in the world. You believe that a certain football team is better than another football team because one has better players. You need to realize that although your opinions are certainly extremely important, they are also just what they are, opinions.

Opinions are what you believe is true about subjective topics. Music, taste and sports are all subjective. What this means is that just because you have an opinion does not mean that it is necessarily true. It does not mean that your significant other, friend or any other person that you are currently in a relationship with is going to share your opinions.

In order to improve communications with your loved ones, it is essential that you are open to their opinions, and are accepting of the fact that they may not share yours. Maintaining an attitude of superiority based on your own opinions is going to seriously impact your ability to communicate in a manner that is effective and efficient.

Mind What You Say and How You Say It

Words are important. They possess weight and they affect their recipients. Your words can cut and they can heal, they can prop people up or shoot them down. All in all, words are weapons as well as medicine. Weapons can be used to defend people, and medicines in the wrong dosage can kill people.

What all of this means is that you should think about what you say before you say it. By saying something, no matter how insignificant it is to you, you might be hurting your significant other. The best policy in this situation is to imagine how you would feel if somebody said something similar to you. Don't adopt a high and mighty point of view and pretend that nothing you say is hurtful. Be honest with yourself and realize where you are going wrong in the way you are communicating with your significant other.

Apart from what you say, you should also be careful about how you say it. This ties in with the previous chapter regarding honesty as well. Often, a lot of things simply must be said. If your girlfriend is being too clingy and is not giving you enough time yourself, you definitely need to tell her. This is important because the two of you need to spend a significant amount of time together. Not letting her know that something she is doing is bothering you will end up poisoning the relationship, as you will begin to resent her for doing something you dislike.

At the same time, it is very important to understand that the way you tell her that what she is doing annoys you is also very important. Your tone, the way you approach the topic; all of these are an essential part of the message you send. If you are overly harsh, it could end up harming your relationship and making the situation worse than it already was.

Focus on a Thing at a Time

Discussion and communication is essential to the health of a relationship, this much you probably already know. Often, when communication has begun to wane between two people who are in some sort of a relationship, it is important to sit down and have a discussion and talk about anything and everything that each of you feels is affecting the relationship.

This is a great way to get past certain things that either of you might find annoying, hurtful, or to discuss things that each of you find pleasant. This allows you to humanize each other, to gain a deeper level of understanding regarding each other's likes and dislikes as well as what each of you wants from this relationship.

However, whilst having a discussion, it is also important to realize that you cannot let the conversation meander through a variety of topics. You need to be concise and be focused. The thing is, communication is great. It is literally the only way to let other people know what you want. However, communication without a single focus can often lead to the problem at hand never being discussed properly. Hence, when you talk to your significant other, it is important that the two of you maintain a single topic of discussion until that topic has been exhausted after which you can move on to the next topic.

Focus on what's Similar

While you are communicating with your significant other, you will come across a huge amount of differences between the two of you. This has been mentioned before in this chapter in the section regarding arguments. Arguments are certainly where a lot of discrepancies in personality and opinion will lead.

However, in order to successfully communicate with your significant other and successfully continue your relationship, if in fact that is what you wish to do, it is very important that you try your best not to focus on these arguments alone.

Everybody has his or her differences. However, the fact that the two of you are in a relationship means that you obviously have some similarities as well. There are probably positive aspects to your relationship along with the negative. Otherwise you wouldn't be in a relationship in the first place.

In order to communicate better, you need to see past the negative aspects of your relationship. Focus on the positives as well, and you will surely see an improvement in the way you communicate.

Don't Make Assumptions

Communication is how you find out what your significant other is feeling or thinking. However, it is extremely common for people to simply assume that someone feels a certain way about something when in reality the opposite is true. Obviously, the person that has made the assumption has no idea how the other person feels. Yet they feel as if they can ascertain their entire emotional profile from a single expression they make, or their tone of voice or loudness level as they speak a single word.

Never make assumptions about what somebody else is feeling. Never make assumptions about what somebody meant by saying a particular thing. This is one of the greatest impediments to effective communication because it is literally the opposite of effective communication. Making assumptions means that there is a complete lack of any form of communication whatsoever.

If you find yourself making an assumption regarding how your significant other is behaving, just approach them and talk to them. Communicate. Ask them why they said what they said, or if they really feel the way you think they do about something that you said or did.

Communication is all about connection. Don't sever the connections that you can enjoy because of your ego. Making assumptions often leads to frustration simply because you cannot be completely sure about what the other person is truly thinking unless you ask them. Do yourself a favor. Save yourself the frustration and just communicate with them in the first place.

Accept Your Mistakes

This book is meant for humans communicating with other humans. Chances are, you are a human. In fact, I am certain that you are one. Humans make mistakes. It is what makes us so beautifully tragic and endearing at the same time. Since you are human, chances are that you're going to make more than a few mistakes over the course of your life. This does not make you evil; it just means that you are just as flawed as the rest of us.

A common mistake made in communicating with others is a refusal to accept blame, not acknowledging that there are certain flaws inherent in all of us. Maybe you have a tendency to drink too much, perhaps you have anger issues that you need to sort through, perhaps you are too sensitive and people simply don't know what to say around you. In a relationship, these flaws are going to get in the way of effective communication. However, what is more detrimental to effective communication is a refusal to acknowledge these flaws.

When you refuse to accept your mistakes and flaws you become defensive, you attempt to victimize yourself and, in doing these things, you build a wall around yourself, a wall that prevents you from communicating with your significant other or from them communicating with you. In order to begin communicating more effectively, learn to accept yourself for who you are, acknowledge your mistakes and try to work on them.

No Interruptions

There is nothing that disturbs the flow of a river more than stones thrown into it at regular intervals. Although the stones may seem insignificant, over a period of time they can actually begin to alter the way the river flows. A large enough build up of stones can stop the flow of a river entirely.

In this analogy, the river is communication and the stones are interruptions. Interruptions are the bane of good communication, because people tend to get into a flow when they are talking about something and unnecessarily interrupting them results in them getting distracted. They therefore become unable to articulate what they were trying to say as efficiently as they were doing before. This is very frustrating, which leads to resentment, which leads to a further breakdown in communication.

Often, interjections in conversation are a welcome thing. As long as they are positive interjections that tell your significant other that you are actually listening to them, like statements of agreement, suggestions and so on, they can actually lead to an improvement in communications between your significant other and yourself.

Interruptions, on the other hand, usually occur during an argument or a discussion of flaws or mistakes. If your partner is trying to communicate something, you need to hear them out all the way. Listen to everything they have to say, understand what it is they are saying. Finally, when they are done, you can respond.

Prefer Face-to-Face Interaction

We live in a largely digital world. The vast majority of human interaction now takes place through the use of technology. We see each other via video calling apps, we listen to each other over the phone, we stay in touch through social media but by far the most popular method of communication these days is text messaging.

Text messaging is ostensibly an improved version of letter writing. However, in writing a letter, tears can fall on the page. Handwriting can describe the emotions of the writer, and a personal touch is always added. Text messaging, like all modern forms of communication, is largely sterile. Almost no emotion can be displayed via texts, which leads to a lot of assumptions and guesswork, which in turn leads to frustration and a breakdown in communication.

Hence, it is absolutely essential that you communicate with your partner face to face. Face to face interaction is how human beings were always meant to communicate. It is important that you place emphasis on face to face interaction because it is only when meeting someone face to face can you see their expressions, truly hear their voices and the tones in which they speak completely free of all forms of electronic modulation.

Communication is easy over electronic devices. You just type something out and send it. The vast majority of cues that we get from face to face interaction are not there. It is only through attempting the difficult way, the right way, can you improve your communication skills.

Pay Attention

This section is very similar to the one regarding not interrupting. The thing is, people want to communicate. Your significant other wants to tell you about her day. She wants to tell you about her hopes and her dreams, she wants you to know what she thinks of you and she wants to know what you think of her as well. If there is a problem in communication and it's not with the other person, it's probably with you and is most probably caused by not paying attention to what the other person is saying.

People want to feel gratified. They want to feel as if the things that they are saying matter and that they are being listened to. They want to feel like their words mean something to the person they are speaking to. As you already know, interruptions are absolute no go areas. At the same time, you cannot simply be talking to your significant other and not listening to them speak.

People very frequently begin to daydream when a conversation is underway. When it is not your turn to speak, you probably begin to think about other things because you feel as if what is being said is, for some reason, not important. You need to pay attention, and you need to listen. If you want to improve the way you communicate, it is absolutely essential to do this in order to make the other person feel as though their opinions matter.

Honesty is Key

You simply can't have a relationship without honesty. After all, how can you even hope to trust somebody that lies to you? Similarly, you cannot expect other people to trust you and communicate with you when your communication with them involves deception and dishonesty.

Often, dishonesty involves not lying but simply not being straightforward about what it is you want out of the relationship. If your significant other wants to talk about getting married and you aren't ready, you might avoid the topic or change the subject. This is a terrible way to go about it. Eventually you are going to have to tell your significant other what you think of this relationship.

Additionally, not all dishonesty is evil. There are such things as white lies, after all. These small lies can be about anything, from sexual performance to what you think about the other person's parents. Remember, honesty is important in a relationship. No matter what it is, if you feel you have to lie about to save yourself from going through uncomfortable conversations then you must not lie; you must tell the truth.

However, keep in mind that you shouldn't be honest in all situations. As has been stated in the chapter regarding honesty, if the lie you are telling will keep your loved one from experiencing unnecessary pain, then you are justified in your deception. Do not make a habit of dishonesty, as it is a huge impediment to successful communication.

Do Not Delay Communication

If you feel like something is wrong, you absolutely have to talk about it. Unless there are circumstances that mean that you simply cannot speak to your significant other at all, there is no reason to delay communication.

Once you start experiencing a problem with any aspect of your life, it starts to create an aura around you. This aura is one of tension and stress, and it will almost certainly affect your relationship as well. Your significant other will be unwilling to communicate with you because they will feel as though they are causing this aura.

You absolutely cannot let this happen. If something is wrong, it is essential that you tell your significant other. Let them know whether they are the cause of the problem or not, and tell them as soon as possible. Otherwise your problem will fester into something that might result in the end of your relationship.

Learn to Forgive

You cannot communicate with your partner if you feel as though they he/she has wronged you. However, you need to realize that he/she makes mistakes and has flaws just like you do. The section regarding acknowledging your own flaws also means that you need to acknowledge the flaws of others and be willing to forgive them for it.

Holding on to grudges means you will begin to see everyone as an enemy. This is going to greatly impact your communication skills in a negative way.

Savor It

There are many people out there that attempt to rush through conversations because they feel that it is something that they need to get over with as soon as possible. This is actually the opposite of what you should do.

Speaking quickly will technically finish a lot of the conversation faster than it would otherwise, but it will leave almost nothing said properly. This is worse than a lack of communication. This is miscommunication.

You need to speak slowly. Encourage your partner to do so too. Savor the words you say and make them count. Doing so will help you communicate like never before.

Chapter 10

How to Communicate Better in a Business Environment

Communication is a process of conveying your ideas and your point of view to other individuals. In this regard, communication is not just a one sided process, since it also includes listening to any ideas, problems and suggestions that others might have and then acting on what has been said. This is an essential factor that is required if you ever hope to function in a business environment.

You may now be wondering, what exactly is a business environment? Well a business environment is a term generally used to describe situations that fall within a company's operations. This includes a pretty much every aspect of a business's dealings. Clients, suppliers, the competition, the owners, changes in the legal framework of businesses and market trends all constitute the business environment.

Since there are so many entities that must be interacted with within the business environment, it's no wonder that communication is such an important asset to the successful businessman or corporate climber. Communication is perhaps the single most indispensable component of the business environment in this way. If one is unable to communicate successfully, how can one fix this and begin to communicate in a manner that is more successful and efficient? How can one improve communication skills pertaining to the business environment? Here are some of the steps involved in this process:

Know Your Audience

For starters, you should know the audience you're addressing, because once you know your audience, it makes getting your ideas and opinions across much easier. Different audiences require different styles of communication.

A more reserved audience will require a more reserved manner of speaking. In general, corporate clients tend to be quite efficient in this respect. They demand a sense of austerity, which means that during your presentation, you need to be especially formal while addressing an audience.

Then, of course, there are situations where being informal and jovial is very important. If you are in a managerial position, you will often have to communicate with your employees in a manner that is informal in order to make you appear approachable to them.

Hence, it is clear to see that the way you communicate is very important depending on what kind of audience you are facing.

Different Methods of Communication

There are two ways of communicating

- Verbal communication: This includes all manner of speech as well as written communication. This includes all of the skills that help in sharing ideas, views and discussions, cooperation and one's ability to complete tasks at hand that involve speaking or writing skills.

- Non-verbal communication: Non-verbal communication includes one's posture, body language and gestures. Also, how one dresses and presents him or herself in front of an audience matters. A lot of non-verbal communication is unintentional; it is the direct result of one's particular personality. However, you can attempt to change this by intentionally adding non-verbal cues to the way you speak, such as adopting authoritative postures and being aware of body language.

Usage of Oral and Written Communication

Oral communication is usually used in a discussion of ideas and in problem solving. In professional environments, presentation matters a lot. Hence, this explains why staff are trained thoroughly to be able to fluently present to their audience.

Written communication is used for sending letters to clients, suppliers and other business officials. This should always be professional.

Usage of electronic forms of communication

Electronic forms of communication play an integral and important role in any kind of business environment. Electronic forms of written communication are either emails or faxes. In simpler terms, these forms of communication are any type of communication that can be transmitted digitally. While you are in an office environment, your job will be to interpret loads and loads of information that will be seeding through several sources. The information will be reaching you manually or digitally. It is quite easy to single out the information that is received manually, however, the same cannot be said for the information received digitally so the person working in the business environment needs to make sure that whatever information is chosen, it's correctly written and professionally presented.

Language used for written communication

Communication is known as the process of delivering a message or a speech through several different ways: ideas, thoughts, emotions and sometimes even body language. Considering how you are in a business environment, the language you should be using to communicate should be a language that everyone can understand. Remember when you are writing to someone, they don't have the clues of seeing you or your body language, so your written communication should always be clear. Read it through before sending it.

Tones Used for Written Communication There are three styles and tones used for written communication that may vary while keeping the audience in mind. These are:

- COLLOQUIAL LANGUAGE: This term is used to refer to any sort of language that is extremely informal. It includes street slang and localized colloquialisms. A good example of colloquial language is cockney English, which is a localized form of English found in urban London. Such language is never acceptable in a business environment. Avoid slang at all costs.

- FORMAL LANGUAGE: Formal language is the most respectful language one can use in written communications. Attention should be paid to spelling and grammar. Fillers such as "you know" and "like" are avoided, and attempts are made to articulate what one is attempting to say in a manner that is clear. Formal language is usually used in the business environment while talking to potential clients or to levels of management.

- INFORMAL LANGUAGE: Informal language is a midway point between formal language and colloquial language. It is often difficult to see the difference between informal language and language that is more colloquial. In general, informal language consists of words that are universally recognized, yet the language is not quite as austere as formal language. Within a business environment, informal language is generally used to converse with members of the team you are in charge of, or members of upper management that don't greatly outrank you. This more casual approach denotes closeness to the people you are writing to.

Keeping the seven C's of communication in mind

The most essential part of written communication is to keep the seven C's of communication in mind before writing anything. The seven C's of communication are as follows:

1. CLEAR: The written text should not be vague and should be perfectly understandable to the reader. The language used should be as transparent as possible, with every attempt being made to use the simplest language that can be used for the purposes of keeping the information that is being recorded as easy to interpret as possible.

2. CONCISE: Since business officials and clients do not have free time on their hands, the writer must keep the text as short as possible without missing out important details. Do not use fluff words, do not over express details or describe things more than is necessary. Write what you need to write, describe if absolutely necessary, and move on. The people you are writing to don't have time to read through volumes of information.

3. CONCRETE: Any information mentioned in the written text should be backed up with evidence or be solid. Try as much as you can to leave out any information that is not one hundred percent correct. There will obviously be situations where you simply will not be able to ascertain whether a piece of information is correct or not, but bear in mind that what you write represents the

company view. In cases where you have to use guesswork, make it absolutely clear that the information is not confirmed and state concisely why you included it in your report.

4. CORRECT: Only correct information should be added to the text. If the writer is unsure about whether the information is correct or not then he or she should not add it or should add a disclaimer.

5. COHERENT: The sentences should be properly structured and coherent. Do not meander and do not digress. Since this is a professional report, exercise a measure of professionalism.

6. COMPLETE: The information present in the text should be complete with all the necessary details mentioned.

7. COURTEOUS: The most important factor is to keep the tone formal and courteous. Showing respect is one of the most important parts of business culture, so if you are in doubt about something you are writing about, be courteous.

Presentation of written text

The written text should be coherent as mentioned above and organized in such a manner so that there is no doubt left in the reader's mind. Everything should be written in a clear concise manner. The structuring of the written text should be as below:

1. Introduction

2. Information

3. Conclusion.

The entire written text should be written in a courteous tone, giving respect to the reader.

Accuracy of Grammar, Punctuation and Spellings

When the writer is writing a written communication, the correct use of grammar, punctuation as well as the correct use of spellings is extremely important. If the readers end up finding any sort of grammatical mistakes or any shady use of punctuation, chances will be that they will stop reading what's important and dwell on the errors. It is highly necessary that the standard of work that is being done is impeccable and up to the international standards. It should not contain mistakes. Do keep in mind that a mistake can cost you a loss so make sure whatever you are writing is hundred percent accurate and to the point.

As you will be writing in English, try to make it as clear as possible and avoid using complicated jargon unless you know the recipient will understand it. Use the type of English that is extremely simple and easy to understand to everyone who has basic reading skills.

Proof read your work

Proof reading is another very important factor in written communication. By proof reading, you will be making sure that whatever you have written is written perfectly and there aren't any unnecessary mistakes present in your work. The perfect way to proof read your work is to read it aloud, although that isn’t always practical.

POINTERS FOR VERBAL COMMUNICATION

Simple use of language

The presenter should always keep in mind the audience he or she is presenting to and the factors that matter are age, gender and the literacy level of the audience. The use of simple language is the best way to present to audience of all ages, literacy level and genders as they will find it easy to understand and there will be no doubts left in their minds.

Importance of contribution

Contributing is also a really important part of verbal communication. Whenever there is a verbal communication is going on, make sure you contribute whenever you feel the time is right for you to pitch in. Do keep in mind that you are not just there to be heard. Listening to others while they deliver their opinions is also very necessary because if you are not paying attention to what your colleagues are saying, you will be completely lost and your contribution will be less valuable.

Keep a professional body language

Body language is as important in verbal communication as anything else. No one would be willing to take you seriously if your body language lacks the touch of a professional, so always make sure that your body language is professional while you are communicating verbally. Keep your posture rigid and if you are planning on moving around, make sure you do it for a purpose. For example, pointing things out on a chart may require you to move. Apart from the entirely professional body language, you can also use positive hand gestures to show how you are fully dedicated to the work you are doing.

Taking Notes

For verbal communication, taking notes is a very important factor. It shows that you are an active listener and also helps in contribution and makes it obvious that you are paying attention to the presenter, which is considered a highly professional attitude.

Chapter 11

How to Pitch an Idea

To create and refine an idea is the main goal. Just having an idea does not help. It does not create any success; it builds nothing further from the idea. Ideas bounce off other ideas. That's the way communication works. People tend to become so smug when they get an idea, their ego takes over and convinces them not to build the idea any further which is always a mistake. Bounce your ideas off others, as combined efforts always pay off.

Considering the fact that 100 ideas can bounce off of a single idea that gives you a lot of scope for improvement. Planning, sketching out the idea, building and constructing takes time and require patience. The foundation of an idea can be easily dismissed and discouraged if you can't back it up by being able to answer questions. A vague idea is fine as long as the specific details are worked out and followed up on. Before presenting a new idea, imagine the questions that will be asked and be ready for them with solid answers that back up your ideas.

You need to know what problems your idea will be solving and to whose benefit the idea is. Selling an idea to others, they will want to know why they should consider the idea and your communication at this stage is vital. Thus, having the idea isn't enough. Have answers ready for those who doubt the idea.

The scope of an idea

The bigger the idea is, the more people it may affect. You can use charts to demonstrate your idea in a clearer manner, so that others can see the same vision. That helps considerably in the negotiation process and aids your communication of that idea.

Working on a chart will keep your team informed and also helps you to keep everyone in the picture as the job proceeds. It also pinpoints difficulties in others tasks. You will find this aids communication with other workers and gives them a very clear picture of the progress of the idea in action.

Apart from the idea itself, one must also focus on communicating this idea to potential clients, or anybody that would be interested in the idea that you have. Being shy or reserved is simply not an option in this situation, you will have to be assertive and you will have to get your message across if you want your pitch to be successful.

The power to the idea

You will have to list down the required recipients of your pitch. This list is cut down to two criteria: People who have power to actually put your idea into action. You could possibly work with a CEO of a company. Your idea can be well constructed and built, with details and budget control, with supply lists and team required but your biggest aim, to reach the CEO, can destroy your hope if you haven't prepared for it. A path to reach every single recipient should also be mapped out.

You have the idea but you also need the backing of your boss, your peers and maybe someone in another organization for that idea to work. Thus, communication with everyone concerned is vital if you want to avoid any kind of misunderstanding. Remember that communication shares the idea and communicating with the right people may be vital to your task.

If you are indecisive about whom to pitch your idea to, ask around. You could have a well-structured idea but until you know who to share it with, it is ineffective.

Some ideas can take weeks or months to be fully prepared. Never worry or tense over the time period unless you have a deadline. If you do have a deadline, always prepare your work so that you are ready in advance, so that if you need to make last minute changes, you can.

Listening to other ideas

If you have an idea, it's a good idea to share it with the right people and remember all the usual rules of communication. Listen to their ideas as they may enhance your original idea. How does your team feel about the idea? What do they think? How do they view the situation? All of these things matter.

What is their perspective? What roles are they interested in? As someone said "The most powerful person in the organization might share none of your philosophy, but the 3rd or 4th most powerful person might. The latter is going to be a better place to start."

This shows just how important communication is to the overall concept of pitching. Listening is a huge part of communication in general, which shows that effective communication is required not just in the act of pitching the idea to prospects, but in the creation of their idea as well.

Structure

This is where you increase your caffeine intake and want to avoid a mirror. Always use Ari Blenkhorn's 3 levels of depth breakdown: 5 seconds, 30 seconds, and 5 minutes. The 5-second level is to refine your idea in order to explain the entire concept in 5 seconds. This does not bore the person questioning you and maintains a professional status. Do not convince yourself that your idea is too complicated or advanced to be explained in 5 seconds.

The 30-second and 5 minute levels come out of the 5-second level naturally. In 30 seconds you can elaborate on what you said in 5 seconds. You do not have to worry about what to say in 5 minutes because chances are you will run out of audience during the first two levels. Some people, however, require written pitches. This gives you a chance to ignore the 3 level rules and simply write in complete depth.

As long as you have the right material and resources, you will achieve what you described in 5 seconds. Sometimes having a peer/partner can make things easier. Pitching will be easier as a team because, keeping aside the level rule, if you forget or panic, your partner will be there to further guide the questioning audience.

Testing

The longer you stick with your idea, the more your ego is likely to let you down. Find people to test your ideas on because they can help you to see any flaws or to improve your idea. Get them to ask you questions because there may be questions you didn't even think about that alter your perception of the idea.

If you have to pitch an idea and are worried about your approach or your communication skills, practice in front of a mirror and then try it on family members to see how they accept what it is that you are proposing. If they know that it's so that you improve your work position, they will be happy to help.

When it comes to actually pitching, do not hesitate. If you are well prepared the actual pitching takes very less effort. People who find the need to use tricks and manipulation are usually those whose egos are too big. Do not worry about the pitching as long as you are calm and direct. Also, be willing to listen to others. Listen to their questions and do not rush into answering questions without understanding the full implication of the question.

Learn to accept failure because not all business ideas will work. The communicator who can accept failure leaves themselves open to new ideas and that's always healthy. Listen to what others have to say and use that to help you to realize other ideas that are more valid and acceptable to everyone. The thing with this is that when you put trust in other people's ideas as being better than yours and give them credit for it, you increase your professionalism and your communication skills at the same time.

When all fails, the best option is to do it yourself. A lot of books are self published and businesses have started out small and been made larger. Low budget films have become successful and designers that believed in themselves have really made a name for themselves through that belief in their own ideas. It is very possible that your ideas are good and if you have the finance to back those ideas and believe in them enough, going independent may be your only alternative. Do not feel that your idea being rejected should stop you in your tracks.

Chapter 12

How to Get Over Stage Fright

The fear of performing on stage is relatively common. In fact, most people feel a degree of nervousness and apprehension when getting ready to perform in public. However, if you are nervous to the point where you start to dread facing your audience and are filled with discomfort and anxiousness at the thought of being in the public eye, or at being the center of attention, you might be experiencing a form of acute stage fright.

To deal with or to overcome your stage fright, you first need to assess what exactly it is that you're trying to fix. As with most phobias, there are degrees of stage fright and unless you figure out your trigger or the extent to which you are affected by your fear, you won't be able to fix the problem.

Performance anxiety and phobias of this nature are the top most common phobias in the United States. There are many forms of stage fright. Common and treatable forms include performance anxiety. Stage fright is a form of performance anxiety. Some people, whose career demands it, need to deal with stage fright on a common or even daily basis. You may be a seasoned actor or musician but being on the stage in front of others can fill you with anxiety. An athlete, no matter how senior or well trained, may falter while performing in the public eye because he/she may be experiencing some form of stage fright. From this, one might deduce that stage fright does not necessarily have to include any form of verbal communication at all. Athletes, dancers, etc. can also experience this uneasy phobia and there is no verbal communication involved in these professions.

Stage fright or performance anxiety is quite treatable if the people suffering with it have an open mind about it. People with stage fright try to avoid performing/appearing on stage if they can help it because their fear limits them and starts negative emotions in their mind. They view stage fright as an impairment and fear that they cannot overcome the problem.

Individuals may have different triggers. Stage fright can be neatly divided into four categories.

- People who are acutely fearful of being on stage and go out of their way to avoid it. This sometimes means that their stage fright starts dictating the choices they make in life. They may avoid taking classes that interest them, as they fear they may be discussion based or feel that they may at some point have to take the stage during the course.

- People who don't let their stage fright dictate their life choices, but are nevertheless anxious about appearing on stage and never feel secure and fully confident in the situation. For example, you are nominated to make a toast at a wedding. While you may feel anxious about making a mistake, saying the wrong thing or even appearing stupid in front of a crowd, you understand the delicateness of the situation and speak up in spite of your fear, however uneasy you may feel.

- People whose professional success calls for them to speak or perform in public even if they'd rather not. For instance, an extremely successful businessman may have to address potential entrepreneurs and their form of stage fright may cause them to resent speaking.

- People who work with creative expression such as artists, standup comedians, actors and athletes. While they may

> be good at what they do they are not immune to stage fright. They may yearn to flaunt their creativity in front of an audience but may be conscious about how the audience will receive them.

Solving the problem is a long and arduous process. The first step to solving a problem is understanding it, and that is what you do by breaking stage fright down into four categories. By doing this you are able to digest your stage fright as a smaller problem thus making it a lot easier to understand. You may even fear that your voice will not carry sufficiently for the space that you need to speak in.

Now that you have successfully understood what stage fright is, you can begin to heal yourself and get over it. Stage fright is a huge obstacle to successful communication. It does not just apply to the stage; it applies to all sorts of high-pressure situations such as board meetings, presentations, even asking a girl out on a date. Indeed, for a lot of people for whom communication is not their strong suit, any form of communication whatsoever would be marred by crippling stage fright.

Hence, in order to begin communicating in an effective manner it is important to get over stage fright. Here are ten tips you can use to help yourself do that:

- Focus: or rather, shift the focus. Stage fright tends to be as debilitating as it is due to the fact that we fixate on it so much. When we are attempting to communicate, we should focus on the task that we are attempting to do rather than focus on how nervous we are doing it. Focus on the words you say and how you say them. Your stage fright is there no matter what, paying it so much attention is not going to do anybody any good, least of all you.

- Don't think about what might go wrong. Instead, focus on what you have to get right. Anything can go wrong at any time. Even problems as massive as an earthquake can occur while you are attempting to ask that beautiful girl out, and there is absolutely nothing you can do about it. You might think that this is worrying, but in fact the opposite is true. Since you can't do anything about it, why worry about it? Instead, you should try to focus on things that will calm you. A lot of people use meditation before speaking to help to create calm.

- Avoid self-doubt: as you approach the situation where you are going to have to communicate, chances are that you are going to be racked with self-doubt. You are going to think about all of the negative things about yourself. These things might be your weight, your face, your hair, your voice or any aspect of yourself that you are, for some reason, conscious about. All you have to do is refuse. Refuse the self-doubt entry into your head space. Focus instead on the task at hand and within no time you are going to effortlessly begin to communicate.

- Meditate. As stated above, one of the most effective ways to calm yourself before you have to undertake a momentous communication moment is to meditate. Meditation calms you and clears your mind. It allows you to think about what you need to be thinking about. Alternatively, you can do anything that involves deep breathing and you will be surprised at just how calm it makes you. Exercise has the added advantage of filling up your brain with serotonin, a feel good chemical that will help you feel elated and excited, which will help you overcome your stage fright and self-doubt.

- Stay healthy. A lot of stage fright isn't just psychological. Your lifestyle has a huge impact on how nervous you get when you are on stage, whether the stage is metaphorical or literal. One of the biggest contributors to stage fright is what you eat, or more accurately what you drink. Caffeine makes you jittery, so avoid it as much as possible before getting on stage. Alcohol may make you feel calm superficially, but it is only going to deaden your senses, which will make it even more difficult to focus on the task at hand. Additionally, sugar has the same effect on stage fright as caffeine so avoid it at all costs.

- Picture success. You are a strong person; believe that. Nothing is more crippling to successful communication than self doubt. No one is perfect at communication, so you don't have to feel ashamed about the fact that you are, in some way, not as effective at communicating as everybody around you. Picture your success, imagine what it will feel like when that girl says yes, or when your boss smiles in approval. Whatever happens after you finish communicating, picturing success will at least help you get through the process of communicating itself.

- Practice: that's right. Even if your stage fright has nothing to do with an actual play being performed on an actual stage, there is nothing better than practice to help you get through something that you are nervous about. No matter what it is that you are going to be saying or whom you are going to be saying it to, try to write a script of what you are going to say and practice it. Try to practice out loud in front of a mirror. This will allow you to see yourself and notice any aspects of your posture or body language that you find less than top notch. You can alter these aspects of yourself then and there, allowing you to be confident when you finally get to the big moment and start communicating with the important people in your life.

- Connect. Whoever it is that you are talking to, it is important that you connect with them in whatever way you can. Before you speak, look them in the eye and smile. This makes you seem more human and is something that will help you overcome the barriers to communicating effectively that exist for you. The basic logic behind this is seeing the person you are communicating with as a human, not as an obstacle that you need to overcome.

- Mind your posture. Often people don't react well to what you are saying. This often compounds your stage fright and increases it exponentially. However, the other person's reaction to you is often not because of what you said or how you said it but because of your posture. Do not invade people's personal space. Try to stand an arm's length away while talking. Additionally, look them in the eye, adopt a posture that is warm and welcoming and speak in even tones.

- Accept yourself. You are the best you that you can be. Nobody is perfect, not you and not the person that you are going to talk to. You will never be perfect, and that's okay because perfect is boring. Accept your flaws and remember that trying to be like someone else will make you come across as disingenuous. The best course of action is to just be yourself.

Conclusion

Communication is a vital aspect of the world we live in and there's a very strong argument that it's the greatest desire that any human being has for themselves and for those around them. Communication opens doorways and it helps us to understand the world that we live in. We don't want to spend our lives looking at others and feeling like outsiders, so communicating with them is going to be our only option. If communicating plays such a crucial role in the world that we live in, shouldn't we be the best at it that we can be? I think that's absolutely the case.

You should approach the world that you live in with a sense of wonder and excitement so that you can't help but engage in it. In this book, I hope that I have given you the courage and the desire to really get out there and start getting to know everyone that you can. Whether you're looking for friendship, love, power, or wealth, communication is going to be an obstacle for you on the road to achieving what it is you want. Don't be afraid to really get aggressive with life and go for everything you desire. You should never let fear get in the way of what it is you want from life.

So, in conclusion, I want you to really take away from this book what it means to be really focus on communication. Whether you're talking or listening, I want you to really focus on the world around you and to take away from it everything that you want. Have the dedication and the willingness to invest yourself in someone that you don't know and take away everything that you can from that relationship with them. Don't be afraid to get out there and let the world see who you are. Be brave, put away your electronic gadgetry and start talking.

P.S. Continue your education on the next page...

- Complete Your Business Relationship Skills Education With a Click Away:
- Management: Golden Nugget Methods to Manage Effectively - Teams, Personnel Management, Management Skills, and Conflict Resolution
- Communication: Golden Nugget Methods to Communicate Effectively - Interpersonal, Influence, Social Skills, Listening
- Leadership: Elevate Yourself and Those Around You - Influence, Business Skills, Coaching, & Communication
- Take Your Business Skills Further for Financial Freedom or Corporate Dominance:
- Small Business: EXACT BLUEPRINT on How to Start a Business - Home Business, Entrepreneur, and Small Business Marketing
- Marketing: Golden Nuggets to Market Effectively - Internet Marketing, E-Commerce, Advertising & Web Marketing
- Sales: Foolproof Method to CRUSH Your Numbers - Selling, Sales Techniques, and Sales Strategy

www.ingramcontent.com/pod-product-compliance
Lightning Source LLC
Chambersburg PA
CBHW070850180526
45168CB00005B/1759

* 9 7 8 1 5 1 9 1 1 5 9 5 9 *